Short Takes

BY

MICHAEL MELTSNER

Quid Pro Books

New Orleans, Louisiana

Originally published in 1979 by Random House, Inc., New York, and simultaneously in Canada by Random House of Canada Limited, Toronto.

Published in 2012 by Quid Pro Books.

QUID PRO, LLC
5860 Citrus Blvd., Suite D-101
New Orleans, Louisiana 70123
www.quidprobooks.com

ISBN 1610271149 (pbk)
ISBN-13 9781610271141 (pbk)
ISBN 1610271157 (ePub)
ISBN-13 9781610271158 (ePub)

Grateful acknowledgment is made to the following for permission to reprint previously published material:

Harcourt Brace Jovanovich, Inc.: Excerpt from "George Orwell and the Politics of Truth" in *The Opposing Self* by Lionel Trilling. Copyright © 1952 by Lionel Trilling. Reprinted by permission of Harcourt Brace Jovanovich, Inc.

Front cover image © by Oscar Martínez Heredia. His website is www.oscar.com. mx, where this and other works of art are presented. The author and publisher express their gratitude for the permission to reproduce his beautiful work, entitled "Urban Watercolor," for this cover.

qp

Publisher's Cataloging in Publication Data

Meltsner, Michael.

　　Short takes / Michael Meltsner.

　　　　p. cm.

I. Fiction—United States—Lawyers.

PZ4. M531 48S 2012

813.5'4 79-4778

CIP

Short Takes

Also by Michael Meltsner

Cruel and Unusual: The Supreme Court and Capital Punishment

The Making of a Civil Rights Lawyer

In Our Name: A Play of the Torture Years

To Jessie and Molly

And to the abstraction they remained committed for a long time to come. Many are still committed to it, or nostalgically wish they could be. If only life were not so tangible, so concrete, so made up of facts that are at variance with each other; if only the things that people said were good were really good; if only the things that are pretty good were entirely good; if only politics were not a matter of power—then we should be happy to put our minds to politics, then we should consent to think!

—Lionel Trilling

Tell all the Truth but tell it slant—
Success in Circuit lies.

—Emily Dickinson

Contents

Short Takes

Mr. Baker

THESE STAGGERED, restless flashes begin outside the emergency room of Beekman Downtown Hospital. The chairs here are bright-colored molded plastic, the kind that oppress weary travelers in airports and bus stations. My buns are settled on the rim of an orange cup, the small of my back searching for the factory's idea of support. Salvatore, my assistant on this case, a student soon to be turned out to the wolves, has already given up on the chairs—though his neat, lithe body ought to be exactly what the industrial designers had in mind with their concept of one size fits all. Ever since the nurses shooed us away, Sal has been hunched against the wall, immersed in a casebook entitled *Conflict of Laws*, oblivious to the sounds that drift from the emergency room whenever someone passes through the heavy doors that separate us from my client. Secure for the moment in his academic garden, he accepts that I will do the worrying for both of us.

We rode the ambulance, helped the attendant lift the trolley with the semiconscious Mr. Baker to the concrete ramp, and followed the body to a hospital bed. Ever since, Sal has been steadily withdrawing. He is no stranger to hospitals, having been a medical corpsman in Vietnam; it was there that he learned the closed-heart massage that may have saved Baker's life—that is, if Baker wasn't just taking a fall for the audience. The memory of those army hospitals may be working on him. He certainly has no interest in conversation, though neither do I. My mind is occupied with whether Baker is putting on an act, simulating acute coronary insufficiency to go with the clinically established evidence of myocardial necrosis clearly revealed by his medical history.

It is both my shame and my skill that I question this heart attack. There's the rub. He is my client; I am supposed to be his champion. Not only that: the medical records are full of episodes of chest pain induced by emotional stress. Electrocardiograms and blood chemistry reveal abnormalities that cannot be phonied. Baker's desire to escape the judge who was about to send him to prison does not explain the courtroom seizure. There is no doubt except the doubt I feel.

Of course, Obitan labeled him a fraud the minute the body crashed through the chamber door. Maybe I'm still prone to the notion that judges

1

know something I don't.

With that special tenacity of the student returned from the wars, Sal has done his legwork, but his report of Baker's rise and fall fails to stamp him noble or base. Is he hero or hustler? It might make good copy, though by this time we've all read the story before: a youth spent dealing and running numbers, in and out of state training schools, graduation to suburban burglaries that were unusual only in that they were impelled by a system. No one bothers any more to plan crimes; even then Baker showed signs of a special gift. He and his accomplices rode early-morning trains north with domestics from the Bronx and Yonkers. They made friends, teasing out the habits of the employers by flirting on the 8:30 to Scarsdale. Later they would arrive at an empty house with a van and in an hour whisk it clean of all fencible items. Returning from Stowe or St. Thomas, the owner would find his house bereft of appliances, jewelry and loose cash. So gentle was the wooing of the maids that no connection was ever made between these early-morning courtship patterns and the slick burglaries. According to Baker, they were a cautious lot. To make certain the M.O. wasn't discovered, the team regularly shifted train lines: first the Croton-Harmon, then the Harlem division.

It was Malcolm X who reformed him. Baker's soul, ready to be saved, put up only the briefest of struggles. He had been drawn to the backroads of Westchester by the lure of travel in a foreign land. Once there, he observed a social fact—the exposed suburban house—and everything else followed. He jived the domestic, waited for the inevitable vacation trip, arrived with the empty truck from R. B. Cesspools and Septic Tanks and returned to the city for a quick sale. To Baker it was a living like any other. "It kept me off the streets," he said. But even before Malcolm's glare, he began to tire of the game. Perhaps it was the need for system: the repetition required for success was too much like work, something Baker had little experience with, but enough to know—at least then—that he wanted no part of it.

Malcolm sized him up immediately. The great man stared Baker up and down and called him a puppet of the white man. "He looked into me like a shop window and said straight out what he saw." There was no discussing these assessments. Men like that don't bargain; if you argued, you could go to hell. "Listen, brother, get off the dime or you're a dead man. If the cops don't kill you, some dude with a knife will. Shuck it."

Baker heeded the master, though death worried him less than becoming one of the men on the corner—trembling, shuffling, tumored, clutching bottles in paper bags. He joined the Muslims and after Malcolm's assassination enrolled in the chaotic world of the New York Panthers, where they talked of bombing department stores one day and free breakfast programs for undernourished urchins the next. But it wasn't until he became director of an East Harlem health center, one of those anti-poverty programs the city planted in the sixties without knowing whether they grew in sun or shade, that he found his stride, the right mix of local anarchy and official approval. By the time the cops arrested him for embezzling government funds, he had parlayed control over a small payroll into considerable neighborhood influence. It was thought that if any black who was accessible to "just folks" could fix something downtown—a building permit, a summer job—it was Baker. He denied this to me, huge teeth flashing a smile to let me know he wasn't offended by the suggestion, and replied cautiously that he never used what little influence he had for other than advancing community projects.

When Baker walked down Third Avenue, shopkeepers greeted him with gusto. The kids respected him even though sometimes he wore a suit. He seemed to live in his office and didn't even own a watch. Thus the charge they got him on adds to the mystery. The state's lawyers claimed that Baker was diverting federal money to unauthorized purposes, and Baker agreed that technically they were correct. He replied—and insisted on a jury trial to demonstrate—that he spent the money to strip lethal lead paint from tenement walls, to repair dilapidated playgrounds, to pay kids to remove garbage that the Sanitation Department ignored—all discernibly related to the neighborhood's health, which after all was his domain.

The street story is that Baker kills arsonists and that "they" caught him for taking some crumbs because the murders are unprovable. When I defend Baker's peculation, this gossip concerns me not at all; when I try to understand the quantity of goodness left in the world, to judge, the inadmissible evidence is crucial. Here again I know almost nothing, since Baker used his dying heart, his history of angina, as an excuse to change the subject whenever I tried to slake my curiosity. The fact is, the incendiary curse of the slums, whether set by absentee landlord, disgruntled lover or bored gang, is almost unknown in the health center's cachement area. Too many charred bodies have been found, immolated by their own jerrycans.

I have no way of telling and don't really care whether he picked up a few crumbs for his flock, lined his pockets or even supervised the murders. About the client of a defense counsel, I don't care; about the man, his essentials, the divination of his...direction, where the scale tips, I do care, and care more now that I've talked to Slade.

Earlier this afternoon, when I met Baker at court, I went over the humble-pie speech we'd worked out the week before. He was shaky—in fact, more humble-pie than I'd ever seen him—but I still worried that he wouldn't show Obitan enough deference. Baker stands six feet four. He is as lean and muscular as a National Basketball Association guard and usually has the air of a savage who eats baby dolls for breakfast. But in the emptiness of the cavernous courthouse hallway, on this the day of his sentencing, Baker looked more the miserable native captured by slavers. Slouched on a bench, shrunk to half his height, he had a mournful cast to his deep brown eyes. Perhaps he could get away with it.

"Work with your weakness," I said. "That's right, think midget. This judge regards you as an arrogant colored man."

Baker responded by meekly dropping his head between his knees, as if he were about to lose his lunch on the marble floor.

"Great. Keep it up." I walked across the hall to check on Obitan's movements. He was still charging a jury.

In a graffiti-covered phone booth I kept an eye out for the judge, fished for a document in my shoulder bag and dialed Clare, the lawyer who works with me at the clinic.

Everyone takes Clare as ardent and sincere, but I always listen for the tinkle of a barely audible sarcasm—one that matches my own, only softer.

"Any calls?"

"An ADA who claims you're ducking him, someone who wants to sell you municipal bonds, and oh yes—the White House."

"Who was it?"

"Gatorade, maybe. Or Marmalade. I couldn't get it. Jeremy, aren't you going to tell me what's happening?"

"The Pres is in a big hole. He wants me to fly straight to Moscow, without passing GO."

"Well, whoever it was wants you to call him back."

My talk with Gary Slade was short and painful; afterwards I was stuck with choices I didn't want. Slade had been with me at school. Later we did some consulting for a study commission, joined together to put over a short-lived conspiracy for reform. The pitch was that the two age-old approaches of dealing with dangerous criminals—executing them or holding them in warehouses—helped nobody. Since prison walls weren't about to come tumbling down, our plan was to set up going businesses to be run by the inmates and owned by the long-termers; any profit they made would be split with the victims. It wasn't a lightweight scheme for turning out license plates or computer key punchers, but a chance for real work. The idea never got a hearing: before we'd circulated a memo proposing mature consideration by a subcommittee of luminaries, the union-man realist on the panel killed it by throwing a fit over the jobs his members would lose. I hadn't spoken to Slade since and didn't much like him: he was the sort who talks shop on the tennis court. Nevertheless, we'd be colleagues for eternity, would always return each other's calls. The union man taught us that you don't necessarily do good by being good. His scorn drew blood that had mingled.

Now that he's special assistant to someone or something important in Washington, Slade's time is too valuable for reminiscence. "Listen, pal," he said brusquely. "You're being considered for a federal judgeship. If you want it, get your friends in line. Hustle."

"Thanks, buddy," I began, but Slade didn't even say goodbye; he was already on his next call, probably talking water rights to the governor of Wyoming or tight money with the Federal Reserve.

The prospect of judging urges me to make up my mind whether enough light is left in the law to see what is happening. Most people who know anything about litigation regard it as a fraud. Not that important things aren't decided. On the contrary, it's just that the third-hand stories heard in court are marketed as truth. Lawyers, judges, the parties themselves must act as if they were certain, as if things were clear. With so much deception in the air, one must navigate by character, and the telltale usually shows nothing but bull. Often I have thought if this is what being a grownup is all about, I'll stay a self-indulgent child.

I'm in a bind. Before I tell about Baker's bizarre behavior, I want to give fair warning. The certified social engineer part of me believes steadfastly that every consumer is entitled to full disclosure, freedom of information, truth in packaging. I'll feel better if I begin by venting a few generalizations, some catch phrases and labels. These stereotypes—why mince words?—are as true as they are false, but this whole exercise will be a waste if the reader is not prepared to follow the twists and turns of what we used to call the New York Lindy. That's the goal, I suppose—approaching both dancer and dance, mastering the mystery without taming it.

Several years ago the flow of cases over my desk began to get to me. Their impermanence threatened my sense of accomplishment. I tried to build a dam by writing books about notorious murder trials. The newspaper reviewers said they were too cerebral. The law journals accused me of popularizing. The books sold poorly, their reception left me without a monument, but at least I acquired a literary agent.

Fritz, my agent and friend, says drop the harshness, tip off the changes, let things glide rather than jump. It's probably good advice, but I can't take it. The jumps are there, the edges are hard. And readers have rights, rights to the gist of what's coming. Otherwise they might respond in the tedious and unproductive manner of what my brothers and sisters at the bar call a cold bench: a panel of judges who haven't bothered to read the briefs so don't know the facts of the case and must badger counsel to fill them in. A lawyer can waste a lot of time with a cold bench, time he doesn't have, just getting it thawed out—telling the esteemed jurists, for example, why the case is in their court.

Rocking back and forth in their government-issue easy chairs, assuming a look of majestic detachment, these unprepared judges peek at the official case record, thumb through mountains of red-lined motion paper and cumbersome exhibits, all the while peppering the attorneys about preliminaries and peripheral matters. Because a cold bench hasn't done its homework, we servants of the court are called upon to deliver some trivia to get the judges settled in the right groove. Between the obsequious may-it-please-your-honors opening and the no-nonsense command of the red exit light on the lectern, hardly any time is left for law, much less justice. Consideration of mercy, of course, is virtually unknown.

I don't really fault the judges for wanting some of the details spelled out before they decide what may prove doom or destruction to those unfortunates, the clients—if only they'd remember that at most we have thirty minutes of their precious time. Take a case on my personal list of the top ten screwball lawsuits. The Federal Trade Commission ordered a razor-blade manufacturer to withdraw a television commercial passing off as a peach— a succulent and fuzzy one at that—the lathered billiard ball whisked soft and clean by its product. Instead of surveying the murky line between art and artifice, exploring the impact of commerce on the public airwaves, the white-haired tribunal of ice cubes cared only about how the lather held its fluff under the heat of thousand-watt studio lights. The lawyers on that one were tied up by minutiae as neatly as Gulliver.

These side issues, you see, have a certain interest, but to sell our client's story we have to press on to the essentials, to the gravamen of the dispute. (I dote on terms like gravamen because they keep me alert to the fact that I belong to a profession that uses weighty forms of expression—in this case, one that also denotes weighty—where a light one, like gist, would do.) In the old days the search for the gravamen took hours. What with the judges sending clerks out to retrieve dusty treatises from their chambers and the reading aloud of troublesome passages from Mr. Chief Justice Marshall and Mr. Justice Story, the advocates went away with the warm feeling that the court had heard all there was to say and had settled something once and for all. No longer. There are too many disputes, touching every form of human madness, for leisurely reflection. And the rules change while you're looking at them. Judges now are as much part of the machine as anybody else.

In almost two decades of practicing this craft of sharpening while narrowing the mind—as put by Burke, one of those commentators lawyers quote but never read—I have developed a decided preference for a hot bench, eager beavers who begin to hassle me about the core of the dispute before I've settled my notes and cleared my throat. These judges may be no wiser than their chilly brethren, but at least they allow me to feel I've done what I came for, leaving to the always lengthy brief all the unnecessary plot development, character analysis and what Fritz calls the weather. It may be the bias of one who has been hurt, but only a hot bench is secure enough to transcend the material.

In my family we usually assume the worst. We perform best under tension. When a situation seems too loose, it will occur to us to inject some stress. It comes naturally for me to take the offensive and serve notice that this will be one of those oracular, egocentric displays with which lawyerdom regularly befuddles and oppresses the laity. But don't be alarmed. If I'm out to bruise anyone, it's myself. The truth is—though Fritz will be furious that I put it this way—my compass probably won't point far from the comfortable haunts of the same old crowd. We want to see ourselves as originals; more so as the world's supply dwindles. Looking backward, I hope to encounter novelty and a steady percolation of the insight we typically overvalue. But I suspect even strangers spot just another moralizing Jewish lawyer who detests the more-sacrificing-than-thou connotations, a New Yorker who, despite ever-present longings to flee elsewhere, will die here. I live in a part of this ugly, demeaning but eternally agitated city that writers call polyglot—though walls not voices distinguish my neighborhood, invisible walls that keep us jammed together and far apart. (Saul Bellow, that chickenshit, quit and moved to Chicago.)

At the risk of breaking my own rules, let me say also that I am suspicious of words. Unless you're Tolstoy or George Eliot, the fewer the better. Ultimately, words hide more than they reveal. The Wall Street wolfpacks who devil me in court use language to smother ideas, not to convey them; because their verbiage comes in a recognizable package, it is assumed that even a prolixity induced by rates in excess of a hundred dollars an hour must be taken seriously. The inflation of legalese has made litigation uneconomical for anyone who isn't supported by a fleet of corporate jets or an open-ended foundation grant. Remember King Solomon, the baby, and the two would-be mothers? Well, the wise judge wouldn't have seen the women's faces for the procedural objections, the cunning affidavits mooting obscure jurisdictional twists. Truth is so elusive that anybody with a license to dispute can make a good case that reality is an abstraction. Our modern-day advocates, with the wordy accretion of centuries to draw upon, are just as capable of deceiving us as the tenacious rabbinical quibblers of old.

But there are other, more important reasons why I'm wary of words. It is the unnecessary padding of people having to fit their goods into precon-structed containers—movies that must run two hours even though they exhaust our patience after ninety minutes. The substitution of time for metaphor. People feeling that everybody has to get it, even if they have to write down and write out and surrender their quick here-and-gone vision, the vision of the age, for the turgid, lugubrious elaborations of meaning. Spelling things out doesn't necessarily show respect to a reader. I'd rather dart about in confusion than stand around waiting for something to hap-pen.

Baker was given a fair trial, as trials go. Twelve men and women—four of them black and two book editors (as every trial lawyer knows, the most sentimental jurors around)—decided he was guilty. Obitan did us in deftly, allowing all our objections to protect himself from reversal on appeal. Bad vibes do not constitute reversible error. The sole legal taint on the record was Obitan's unwillingness to postpone the trial after Baker claimed his health had deteriorated. By sentencing time we had at least accumulated a hefty file of medical reports attesting that the extreme stress of prison could push Baker over the edge into a fatal seizure.

Sal searched the bodegas and taverns of the barrio, looking for clues to whether Baker was legit. He knew, of course, that even if Baker was just an-other ghetto hustler, we would still put on the same defense. But I wanted to know, and Sal didn't seem to hold this private agenda against me. In fact, he soon made it his own, as if Baker's essential goodness or warp would help strike the balance between the claustrophobia of a Queens childhood and the saturnalia of Southeast Asia. Sal does not talk about the war, though he knows of my interest, and I have decided not to push him. Whatever our different reasons, we have become more than Baker's lawyers. The natural bias for or against the client has been replaced by a need to apprehend.

We prepared our sentencing argument carefully, hoping to press Obitan into accepting that Baker's health and record of community service made jail time inappropriate. First we made our pitch to the probation officer, who usually wields the influence in a proceeding of this sort, but we were unsuccessful despite the dossier of character references and medical testi-monials. From the beginning we got a cold shoulder from Obitan. His clerks never looked us in the eye; the bailiff declined to pass the time in small talk. Something had been said in chambers about this case that no one wanted to reveal. I considered the possibility of prosecutorial funny business, but the district attorney was as straight and tight as a violin string. The arson stories might have seeped in some other way. No one does as badly with law enforcers as a vigilante because he challenges their monopoly.

It finally surfaces as something simple and therefore unexpected: old age. On the bench Obitan shows signs of wear and tear. He has been at this work too long. Whether it is senility or distemper or the accumulated frustrations of judicial self-repression, he has moments of growling impatience, others when he seems furious that Baker denied his guilt, putting him to the trouble at his advanced years of holding a trial. The first time we argued that Baker deserved probation Obitan was ready to turn us away and send him to jail; the marshals were itching to grab him. I managed to get the sentencing adjourned on the transparent ruse (No. 14 in the Attorney's Handy Deskbook of Trickery and Confusion) that there were additional medical tests to be brought to the attention of the court, even though the court wasn't the least bit attentive. Gathering Baker's up-to-minute test scores dragged on for months, and when we finally have to show up, Obitan still isn't interested. He latches onto an opaque summary of Baker's condition prepared by a physician chosen from a list of government-approved impartial experts, and starts ranting about the technical language.

"What does *this* mean?" he screeches, scowling at hangdog Baker across the table.

We are in chambers, too close to Obitan for comfort. The DA silently skims his legal file, flipping the pages as if looking for something, though clearly he's hiding from the angry judge's white heat. Two law clerks, a year out of school, lean back in their chairs against the bookcases, subtly dissociating themselves from their master; the clerk of court hunches over his docket; a stenographer, his eyes on the ceiling, listens to the sound and not the sense of the words.

The judge is addressing Baker, who hasn't studied the three pounds of illegible doctor scrawl or been briefed by a cardiologist about his deteriorating condition. In a criminal court my job is to stay between my client and the judge; I try to deflect the question.

"It means, your honor, that he suffers chronic attacks of chest pain and shortness of breath, diagnosed as subendocardial infarction first evidenced in—"

"I asked *him*, counselor. Do you still work?"

"He hasn't since—"

"The defendant, the defendant."

"I get relief now, but previous to the trial I worked for eight straight years."

"What do you have to say for yourself?"

There is no hair on Baker's face or head. He is blackness itself, wearing, in total disregard of my explicit orders, a fierce shark's-tooth necklace that falls belligerently over the embroidery of his orange dashiki. Obitan's mop of white hair reminds me, against my will, that he too was once a child. Beneath the flowing robe, he is turned out in pinstripes and blue broadcloth. Around his scrawny neck is a silky tie in a too-big collar. He looks wasted.

After hearing Baker repeat his claim that he meant no harm, was merely diverting resources under his control from one budget item to another in order to meet crying needs, and profited by not a penny for himself, the judge is ready to sentence. It will be what? Probably six stupid months. I have nothing to lose and once again try to get across my main points: no jail can he trusted to minister to the medical needs of my client; too heavy a prison work detail could finish him; in any event, the circumstances of his crime are not so serious as to justify risking his health and life.

To do this sort of thing right you have to be involved enough to show conviction, and detached enough to observe yourself and everybody else in the room. Sensing anger in the judge ready to rush out and flood the court-house, I talk as briefly and quietly as I can. When I've finished, Obitan leans over his desk and glowers at Baker. For him I am not there.

"You people—"

But the judge never finished.

"Enough." Baker rose from his chair. "Enough of this shit."

For an instant I was afraid he'd lunge across the table and choke the judge where the turkey-gizzard neck met tie and collar. But he merely turned away, the chair falling to the floor. He took three steps—plodding, deliberate steps, while no one else moved—and fell like a toppled pine tree against the heavy door that guards the judge at work. The door popped open, then gently closed to meet Baker's inert body.

Suddenly we were all on our feet. Sal got there first and grabbed Baker by the shoulders to turn him over. Obitan was busy pronouncing judgment. "Phony. Phony baloney. Bull turds." With a wink at the clerks, he ordered: "Call the nurse."

Sal took a moment to check the glazed eyes, then tested Baker's pulse. Finding it shallow, he struck. Had he kicked Baker in the testicles, he could not have frozen the room more quickly than by his abrupt palm blow to the heart. Small in itself, the noise, when combined with the sight, was deafening. Immediately everyone exhaled, as if he had struck us all. He pressed his lips to Baker's mouth, in the respiration technique he had learned in the service, and was still at the body when the ambulance arrived.

Last night my dream began at a butcher-block table set up smack in the middle of Central Park South. A group of us were seated at this table in distinctive bentwood chairs—original Thonets, no doubt. A truckdriver shook his fist and cursed us for blocking the street, but we dealt on. We were playing high-low with consecutive declarations, a game where calling last—high, low or high-low—is important. As my oldest friend Rudy skated the cards across the slick wood, Clare grimaced. With each card she frowned more, letting us know this wasn't her game but she had to play. Gary Gilmore, the murderer, raised every bet. It made a mess of the percentages, but being dead he didn't care. He had half the table to himself while we huddled together; he sat behind slanting steeples of blue and white chips, robust in a black T-shirt with a white cardboard heart pinned to his chest. Though I had a perfect hand—a straight flush and a six-four low—Gilmore rose from the table, scooped the chips into his Stetson and ambled away toward the Plaza. I pointed my index finger at his back. He turned, and we stared at each other across the traffic.

Sal is still hunched over his lawbook. I've made peace of a sort with my chair by curling up like an embryo. An umber lady with squinty eyes, and glasses hanging from her neck by what looks to be a shoelace, comes through the big doors to tell me that Baker is out of danger. I'm ready to go home and sleep it off. If tests confirm that he really had go home and sleep it off. If tests confirm that he really had an attack, I'll use Obitan's brutal remarks as the pretext for a motion to recuse the arbitrary old man from sitting on the case. The arrival of a creative thought, amidst the hospital-induced dullness, and the prospect that Baker may yet outlive his judge rouse me sufficiently to poke Sal with my foot.

"A cab. My treat."

The frugality learned in his mother's kitchen won't allow Sal to accept. "It's faster by subway."

"I'm not interested in speed."

We reach the street, where even breathing pure auto exhaust is an improvement, and catch a cabby heading north. Immediately he gets stuck in a mammoth jam near the Holland Tunnel. We sprawl across the seat.

"Sal, what do you think of judges?"

"Huh?"

"Judges—you know, the fellows in the black dresses. Do you want to be a judge when you grow up?"

"Hell no."

"Why?"

"They sit on their ass all day."

"How about their power to do good?"

"There's that."

"And bad."

"Yes."

"I feel like I'm talking to a typically deferential, respectful and obedient law student—which you're not."

"I was watching Obitan. Muddled and cruel as he is, in a way he was penned in by the rules. I'll bet following the rules changed him and what he does. At least when he was younger."

"You mean he learned things."

"Maybe. But I'm talking about behavior. The system makes him less of a pig than he naturally is. He could have killed Baker. I mean, the man felt like killing him, but the judge had to hesitate—had to find a justification that would stand up in public. He knew he could get away with six months, even more, but he still had to find a reason."

"And a better man..."

"It would cut the same way. A better man would be held back from doing something worthwhile. The law squeezes us together and puts us all in the same boat. That's why I like it."

How can I struggle with jurisprudence in a cab lurching from pothole to pothole up Eighth Avenue? The laws of the United States are flawed but not dishonorable. The pay is lousy but more than I ever earned. With the job comes instant approval from almost everyone I know, deference from those I don't and even a little power. No other clod out there on the pavement, whether a self-satisfied theatergoer rushing to an early dinner or the dregs of the Western world loitering on the Minnesota Strip, would sympathize with a moment's tragic ambivalence. Why hesitate? Judges politic like everybody else. I've spent so many years in the courts that I must like their tunnel-vision view of the world a little. I know the name of every case I've handled; I've played the game, not slavishly but by the rules, and a federal judgeship is like getting to manage the Yankees.

But my head is throbbing. If I'd eaten, I would roll down the window and add the contents of my stomach to the rest of the garbage. I am the only son of an only child. An only child, I submit, is a winner—must be a winner. This is my beacon. Where others are frightened that they are determined by such vital statistics, I exult. What I want will take place. Public doubts, yes; one must have them for form's sake. Private doubts, until recently, have been rare. My cousin Philo says faith healers work. Healers have the gift, the belief in their omnipotence, and its force carries the patient along. But I am sweating in the back of a taxi. Sal is about to ask if I'm all right.

Mr. Baker remains an unknown to the judge I would want to be, the judge who would apprehend before he acted. This judge would not be satisfied with a rationalization when a reason was called for. Decent, demanding work is usually boring, but it frees us to be something; the angst begins when we dare ask what.

A few weeks after I finally delivered him to the marshals, my client sent me a note on the marginless copybook paper the government provides for inmate correspondence. The black lines on the paper reminded me of iron bars, and Baker's calligraphy made each letter look like a tiny person trying to squeeze through.

"Dear lawyer," he wrote. "You did your best with a hard case. Thanks for everything. Now that it's over and we've said our goodbyes, I'd like to know you."

Cards and Horses

THE FIRST SUMMER I worked, we drove north from New York in a used DeSoto, windows rolled down, heat beating up from the asphalt, radio full blast. The car had an immense engine that coughed beneath a sleek, stretched-out hood much too long for the body. The springs bounced, but the seats were faded plush; we felt invulnerable. Pulling into a rest stop on Route 19, the cowboys eased their mounts up to a stream on the Great Plains. Hills in the distance, the country at our feet, we bought Cokes and stood by the car, staring. I wondered what was going on in Shelly's head. Hell, what was going on in mine? City boys staring at a cow, minds turning to mush.

In the Catskills our introduction to the business world was abrupt. Arnold gave us each a checkbook, a laminated identification card, legal release forms, yellow pads and a box of No. 2 pencils. Every morning we'd use a pay phone across the highway from our bungalow to call his girl, Nina, for a list of the claims that had come in the day before. A tennis-court fracture named Cohen at the Cozy Villa. A sprained ankle at the Manor on Route 28, name unknown. A pool slip at the Raleigh (while there, check out cracks in the macadam). Hot soup spilled on Marks at Crystal Valley. A complaint of food poisoning, moldy fruit salad, at the Fairhart Day Camp in Kerhonkson (Arnold wants a good look at their kitchen; the owner is not one of his favorite people).

Shelly was pushing Nina and getting nowhere. Despite her ponytail and corduroy jumper barely hiding rolls of baby fat, Nina was sleeping with Arnold. Shelly wouldn't believe it: "Listen, sport, he's forty-eight years old, five feet four, and wears cuff links. Nina is twenty-two and goes to a teachers college. You have a dirty mind. Let's shoot some hoops."

We'd play horse and twenty-one until the tourists staggered away from their cantaloupe, sweet rolls, cold cereal with fruit, Canadian bacon, eggs, bottomless coffee cups—American plan, of course.

"Guys, always hit 'em after a big feed," Arnold had preached. "Stiffs settle faster with griddle cakes sloshing around their bellies. They never eat like that at home. They feel guilty." He leaned back in his chair and blew cigar smoke over the desk that separated him from his college-boy hired hands.

"Always see the manager first and get the story. Talk to bellhops and life-guards. Then find the guest. Tell 'em Mr. Shmohawk, the manager, reported an accident, and the rules are that all reports have to be checked out."

He was self-satisfied but eager to please; too eager—not as crude a man as he sounded, this Arnold LaBell. I pulled for him despite the cuff links because he took account of our greenness. He promoted a scholarship of people and money. Kind enough to want to get across that he hadn't made a choice, his unspoken line was: fate put me here; what can I do?

"If they ask, say you're from the Hotel Association; never mention Friendship Mutual. *Nevah.*" He pronounced the word the way Bette Davis would.

Arnold made most of his money from the automobile, persuading juries that whiplash was the scourge of the twentieth century. In the summer, when the courts slowed down, he dabbled in insurance. We were his eyes, arms and legs. He never felt quite right when he wasn't making a profit. Put in the desert, he would have found a way to take a percentage on sand. But at least he was cheery, his greed diluted by mockery.

"Then you pull out your pad and get them to tell you what happened. 'I'm gonna take this down in your words,' you say." Arnold held up the pad for emphasis as if we were mental defectives. "You write, 'My name is Sandra Accident-Prone, I am a guest at the Lake Minnihale Club.'" He repeated, "I... am...a...guest," pausing after each word. "'After gulping down two whiskey sours, I tripped over a three-hundred-pound couch in a well-lit lounge, suf-fering minor contusions and no permanent injury,' or whatever they tell you happened. Always write in the first person—that means *I*, for those of you who aren't at Harvard," He slipped Nina a smirk. "When they've fin-ished, ask them to sign. It's their statement, after all. Any questions?" But his look said, "How could there be?"

"Okay, suppose they won't sign. Then act like you don't give a damn, but tell them you must have their initials on each page so your boss will know you actually did the report. You're clean-cut boys; they'll sign."

Arnold's biggest account was the local harness track. He also owned a piece—a license to make money, as they say. In this county he had a piece of everything. His boys earned gold clubhouse passes, slick plastic decals for the parking lot, grand hellos from the Pinkertons. Shelly and I went to the track every night. Even when we had dates, we took them to the races. After dinner we helped waitresses from the hotels set up for the next morning so we could arrive in time for the daily double. At the track women were an encumbrance, asking stupid questions that distracted us from the serious business at hand and, worst of all, betting hunches—their birthdays or cute names. We tolerated them as cover. Even at Shelly's stage of incipient addiction, he recognized the loss of esteem that would follow an explicit declaration of sex second to horses. We should be parked on some out-of-the-way mountain road, unbuttoning gravy-stained uniforms in the immense seats of the dark DeSoto, but there was always action not to be missed in the eighth race.

For Shelly, the track had the appeal of decadence, allowing him to pass as a Runyonesque insider, but I was attracted more by the control. By turning responsibility over to the wheel of fortune and losing any say in the matter, my position was enhanced—like a litigant forced to place the stakes of a dispute in escrow. The truth was, I felt safer with horses than with women. If my evening's calculations went wrong, the track always offered a capsule explanation: a trainer who decided to run without blinkers, a horse impeded in the stretch, a boozing driver.

On Sundays I lay naked on my cot counting up the week's score, rerunning the week's races, vaguely disapproving of myself. Sometimes the voice of a parent asked if this was any way for someone with my future to spend his time. Shelly was not given to Sunday musings. He had little tolerance for introspection except when handicapping; he was happy only in motion. He dragged me off to a delicatessen in a shopping center strung out along the foot of a mountain. We settled down with roast beef sandwiches on puffy poppy seed rolls smeared with Russian dressing and drew black marker circles around the names of the horses we liked in the overnight entries.

"Lady O with Carmine Hutch," he exclaimed. "Sprints the three quarters and then stops, but every fifth or sixth race she keeps going. Always happens when the price is long and she has an inside post. This time the horse comes out of the three slot with two dogs on the rail. Let's wheel her in the double."

Shelly's passion carried me along. Other people's enthusiasms have always fascinated me. The ultimate in acquisition is to use someone else's energy. When we finally hit the track, I left Shelly to his double and bet the longest shot in the field. In our handicapping rivalry, we switched roles. When he calculated, I played the romantic; when I derived a law of history from the welter of detail in *The Racing Form*, he daydreamed and free-associated. He watched the race pogo-sticking up and down, using my shoulder for leverage. A furlong from the finish line he started beating me with his rolled-up program. Wrapped in his joy, we adjourned for steaks.

I had gotten the job with Arnold through the Old Yid network. Shelly's father, Saul, was the super of a fading Broadway palace called the Bay of Naples. The lobby had a mural of Amalfi, a creaky elevator and, on an iron bench, a permanent copy of the *Daily News* always folded so you could see the headline. Saul did construction work on the side for an immigrant named Fenno Bryce, who had been born Isadore Berkowitz. Saul was thin and angular, Bryce was stocky, but their heavy accents were identical. They played in the tradition of vaudeville twosomes, with Saul assuming the Costello-Laurel part to Bryce's Abbott-Hardy. Painting Bryce's apartment on Saturdays, Shelly and I auditioned their who-had-it-worse-in-the-old-country routine. In Vilna they pushed Jews off the sidewalk; in Warsaw thugs roamed the streets, deflowering virgins. Bryce usually won the prize for suffering, his trump the claim that he had escaped from the Auschwitz transit yard.

Saul held his own until Bryce talked of the death camps. With his wife and Shelly, he had bribed his way onto a steamer bound for Cuba. With nine hundred other refugees, they held tourist visas bought at incredible prices. When they arrived in Havana, the gangway was sealed and the Cuban government issued a decree voiding their permits. In the steaming heat the ship began to smell like a toilet. The passengers threatened to throw themselves overboard. The government refused to budge and ordered them to sail. The day before the ship weighed anchor, several passengers took poison; others slashed their wrists. The ship put out to sea, sailing north, the captain stalling for time, waiting for word from a refugee-aid committee in New York. Off Florida they were shadowed by a Coast Guard cutter and warned not to land. The Cubans decided to let the refugees enter if they posted a five-hundred-dollar-a-head bond but withdrew the offer when the ship returned to Havana. Negotiations with the Dominican Republic broke down. Finally, Britain, France, Holland and Belgium agreed to take the Jews in. They returned to Europe. Most were rounded up when the German army swept across the Low Countries into Paris the following year, but Saul had taken his family off at Southampton. Six months later he was working on a boiler in Manhattan.

Shelly and I winked as the two men wrangled; their stories didn't concern us, they might have come from *Grimm's Fairy Tales*. Nothing about Shelly's innocent cowlick of sandy hair, his habit of practicing a private tap dance when no one was looking, suggested an encounter with history. Though he was my best friend, my mother and father had never met Shelly's father. While the radiator hissed, Bryce accused Saul of using green wood on the bookshelves, setting out crooked parquet, covering the house with dust. Clomping around the paint-stained tarpaulin with a spoon dipped in a cottage cheese container, Bryce refused to let us work in peace. Needy for an audience, undeterred by my fantasy of enamel spattering unseen into his lunch, he spouted outrageous demands. He ordered Saul to resand the freshly painted window frames. Saul argued, but only to please Bryce. Their crisp insults had nothing to do with whether Saul actually would do more work on the windows. Shelly asked his father why Bryce hassled him. Saul shrugged it off: Bryce had lost a wife; he, thank God, had been spared. I envied Shelly his past, but he had no interest. When my father talked about the track, Shelly listened carefully.

Bryce's company wrote insurance for the big Catskill and Florida hotels. He described it as the first big Jewish carrier and bragged to Saul that his kid would have a summer job as an adjuster. For personal injuries the Catskills were a high-risk area. In the insurance business, claims, not losses, count most. Whenever a claim is filed, the company has to put money aside to cover it until the courts decide the case seven years later. To come up with cash for the reserves, the company has to borrow. Borrowing costs money. The adjuster's job is to settle promptly every claim short of a cracked skull. It's worth a couple of hundred bucks to write sprains and torn ligaments off the books.

For me, Jewish history is inextricably linked to Hollywood. I watched the Holocaust from the balcony. In one memorable film the Germans burst in while a family of traitors dines on kidneys, their first meat in a year. Even the sedate hausfrau is kicked around. The Nazi officer has no more compassion than his men. He is thin and leather-boy slick. The SS officers arc always thin, probably a theatrical convention going back to Cassius. The soldiers, dressed in clumsy greatcoats, seize the resistance cell, hustle the family off to prison and certain death, but the American airmen go undiscovered, safe in a hidden attic room. Saul's accent and the way he shrugged his shoulders embarrassed his son. I disliked Ernest Hemingway for the way he treated Robert Cohn. There were no hidden attic rooms on Riverside Drive.

It was the terrible fate of those who visited the resorts under Arnold's care to be unaffected by their holiday. Where one might imagine release from the daily grind would free the spirit and allow the city-stifled self to emerge, quite the opposite occurred. In New York there was no choice but to put up with your lot—ride the subways, brush soot from your face, pay the bills. The mountains promised relief, but the resorts merely substituted something called Activities. Sports, games, chasing, mealtimes—all followed tracks straight and inescapable as any encountered by the most servile housewife or working stiff. Activities were summer chores. As if ordered by some invisible alarm clock, husbands commuted, children were delivered to counselors, wives lolled around the pools and overdressed for their canasta tournaments. It may be that the whole concept of a wilderness is flawed, something invented by city people and suburbanites after they lost touch with anything more evocative of the natural world than a rosebush. In the Catskills city ways could not be forgotten: no one went near the woods unless it was to search for a lost golf ball.

Yet the original impulse was to escape the humbling city routine. There were even vestiges of the aristocratic, evidenced by the roadsigns—this way to the Manor, two miles to the Villa, turn left for the Secluded Hacienda—and something of the pretense remained in the heavy tips, two-hour meals, men strolling the grounds with big cigars gently laying the groundwork for business deals they would not conclude until fall, the attempted seduction of any employee within grasp of a bed.

Most of all, the complaints. The complaints spoke of high expectations. Promised something different, led on to expect leisure, French service and the carriage trade, disappointed guests retaliated by bitching. Mattresses were too hard or too soft, roast beef was overcooked or raw. It was humid or buggy or shockingly cool. The rain came down in buckets or the air was parched. In these latitudes a successful hotel manager listened to cries of grief and injustice with the aplomb of a deaf-mute bent on pretending he had no handicap. The failures tried to correct what could not be amended; soon after the Fourth of July they came down with an incurable case of ulcers.

The disgruntled patrons made life miserable enough for the drivers, busboys and desk clerks, the frontliners stationed at the border between paying customers and their winter dreams of transformation, but a whole new order of frustration surged to the fore when they had to deal with me. After all, something *really* had gone wrong. "This vacation has been ruined by the hot coffee spilled on my new taffeta, also scalding my left arm from shoulder to elbow." "... by the severe concussion due to the collapse of warped slats holding up a double bed." "... by the sprained ankle resulting from improper maintenance of the sidewalk connecting the rec hall and canteen." "Ruined" was a word I heard so often that I even lost a bundle on Archeologist, a cheap claimer who would be running still if he had ever started.

Many of these complaints were perfectly valid in both the legal and the moral sense. The equipment was rarely inspected, the college student staff inexperienced and untrained. Certainly negligence coursed the mountains like a plague. I didn't mind the content of the complaints so much as the attitude that went with them. Reinforced by governing legal principles that compensated the injured only if they made a fuss and were free from fault themselves, the attitude transcended actual monetary loss. Someone else is to blame that I am not at the American version of the Château de Mercuès (though they wouldn't have known the name), so pay me. I am entitled to this vacation on the house, so keep the bill, pick up the tab, give me a free ride. It may have made perfect sense legally, but it did something terrible to the participants, including me: it turned life into winning a negotiation.

In the beginning, as I drove the county roads, statement pad and checkbook neatly tucked away in a vinyl zipper case by my side, I had no thought but to serve my master. We spent a day each week talking into a dictation belt arid filling out forms for the main office. Arnold dipped into these files to check our performance—our numbers, as he put it—and afterwards we'd find congratulatory notes written on index cards taped to the dictating equipment, little cheers reading "Stupendo" or "Bombs away."

I didn't figure out until much later that Arnold always found time to praise us for a case that was really a gift (say, where a distraught mother released all claims arising from her daughter's loss of two front teeth in return for our picking up the dental bill) so that he could really dig in and grouch over a blooper—some instance where the file reeked of collusion between hotel owner and guest. Owners were not above subtle suggestions to trusted customers that they carried enough insurance to support almost any claim, so long as the payments were split. Arnold was interested in catching the phonies; apparently it made his summer worthwhile. He didn't care a fig about the good results except as packaging for his educational program, getting the pill of criticism down the hatch.

But from the start I dearly wanted his praise, treasured each "Stupendo," ran into his office like a little boy asking his father, "Did I get it right this time?" As Arnold's squire I approached claimants as if they were the enemy—and I suppose in a sense they were. What they gained, or so it appeared, Friendship Mutual lost. A zero-sum game. Our purposes were cross. Except that I just worked for Friendship Mutual; I was not the thing itself. It was possible for the company to prevail even if I floundered, but it took a while to get this straight.

I badly wanted to win, to win as much in the daytime as on my nightly visit to the track. I worked at it. I studied the importance of concession patterns—the reason given for moving from a hundred to two hundred dollars had to sound convincing. The firmness of my voice, the frequency with which I offered more money, the amounts I jumped, all affected the result. I came to know the thin line between verbal ambiguity and lack of candor, between bluff and lie. There was a time to raise the anxiety level—by silence or stonewalling or the wearisome broken-record tactic that had me repeating the same message until the complainant admitted defeat just to get rid of me. And there was the cultivation-of-trust ploy, a move that worked best with women. I would simply say, "How can I help you? Please tell me what I can do," and they'd turn soft and cooperative.

My favorite tactic—the one that accounted for the quick reputation I picked up with Arnold of having a natural talent for hard bargaining, evidenced by his two "Stupendos" for each blooper—was the "What can I do, I'm in a bind" maneuver. I would simply inform the complainant that I wasn't authorized to go higher than the amount I really wanted to settle for. The timing of this communication was critical. If it came too early, it could scuttle settlement: why talk with a fellow who doesn't have authority? If it came too late, it would look like an afterthought, or, much worse, a trick. People believed you were there to trick them—and, of course, you were—so your actions had to say, "Look, I know you think I'm here to pull a fast one, but it just ain't so."

But there was a time in the dealing, usually after the medical expenses had been computed and this point set aside, after the pain and suffering issue had surfaced and a few words of modest derogation been spoken ("How can we put a value on *that*?"), when I let it be known, in a tone that implied everybody knew, that I couldn't go higher than three fifty. If they wanted to collect a bundle, well, they'd have to hire a lawyer. "It's your right, of course, but let me tell you he usually takes a third off the top, and then there's a wait of about five years." After hearing about lawyers, most of them started talking sense; at this point they conceded that four hundred would do it, and I was home free.

I compiled quite a string of successes operating this way, winning with the complainants and proving myself a better chiseler than my peers. My numbers—which I eagerly checked against theirs on my weekly visits to Arnold's office—stood up even when compared to Shields, the full-time adjuster who worked the hotels year round. When several innkeepers specifically requested that I be assigned to their claims, I knew I'd arrived. This was easy. So confident did I feel, so limitless seemed the future of someone who could turn a profit out of simply giving less than the next guy, that for weeks I daydreamed of Jeremy the Tycoon, snapping out orders, dismissing subordinates, sauntering around a skyscraper office followed by fawning associates and admiring secretaries.

My downfall was both predictable and, I now realize, blessed. It is to my credit that at the time I knew I was due to suffer some necessary adjustment in this world view, one that freed me from the ever-widening prospects of manipulating those around me. One thing about being a horse-player: it teaches you that most of life has the porosity of stone. Naturally,

I was educated through defeat. As Marx and Engels spell out so eloquently, the bourgeois only begins to understand the nature of capitalism when he has been sacrificed to it.

At the main office of Friendship Mutual the push was for total coverage of the mountains. Vast economies of scale were predicted to follow from writing every liability policy in the area. As a result, all sorts of marginal operations had been covered; bungalow colonies, mom-and-pop motels, converted toolsheds rented as woodland cottages, even summer camps— dangerous because they assumed parental responsibilities—were added to Arnold's jurisdiction. At one of these, a seedy collection of cabins barely visible for the unmowed lawn and heavy covering of unpruned wisteria, I met my master and a good whipping.

The case had been in the office for weeks: a particularly long cut on the leg of a thirteen-year-old girl inflicted by the collapse of a defective swimming pool ladder. She had innocently put her foot on the bottom rung to pull herself out of the water, and the screws holding the metal had pulled clear out of the concrete housing. A jagged piece of unfinished metal caught her leg, removing a deep channel of flesh before the whole apparatus sank to the bottom of the pool. As the turquoise water turned crimson, hysteria set in—and continued, I was told, to characterize the family in its dealings with Friendship Mutual.

Shelly had tried first and been told begrudgingly to come back when the girl's father returned on the weekend. Later the father treated Shelly as if he had loosened the screws himself, refused to let him look at the girl's injury and threatened a million-dollar lawsuit to collect damages for her lowered value in the marriage market. He kept saying, "It's a visible scar. It's a visible scar."

Then Shields was sent out, only to be run off the property when for openers he offered to take care of the medical bills. Finally, Arnold turned to me, his record holder, first on the score sheet, lowest dollar-per-claim ratio in the office, rookie of the year. The challenge was obvious. Previously I had handled small-change cases; here was my first opportunity to prove that I really would rule in one of those glass towers where my father had to mug and bow and be someone he wasn't in order to put through his deals. Arnold made a big show of opening the Mosler safe to get the special checkbook that authorized an on-the-spot settlement of up to four thousand. He listened to the tumblers and blew elegantly on his fingertips like a society burglar. Now that I've sat through a hundred more complicated negotiations, I can only wonder if he wasn't pumping up the balloon of my pride for a big pop. But I had no such thoughts then. Arnold was my mentor and could only want the best.

His last-minute pep talk further expanded my authority. "Get rid of it, kid. Use your noodle, but get rid of it."

"Don't worry, Arnold," I replied, like the faithful retainer I was. "I'll bring it in for pennies."

I took the next day off, gathering strength for the assault. Sitting on the porch of my bungalow, chain-smoking Marlboros and stuffing the butts into empty cans of Genesee ale, I plotted the probable bargaining range, the initial positions I would gently hint, the fallbacks I would adopt only if cornered. At six o'clock I ate a dinner of three fried-egg sandwiches and a glass of milk, dressed in a clean white shirt and pressed chinos, and set off for the cabin. Like everything else I planned to do, the hour was chosen with purpose. I hoped for a drowsy opponent, settling into his after-dinner torpor. The hour would also contribute a subliminal communication: it was not only late in the day but late in the summer; unless you want years of hassling with lawyers, let's get this thing over with.

I found no hysteria in evidence. The mother was a small, tired woman; whatever bloom had led her to the altar had long since disappeared. She was dumpy but not old. The girl was homely and dark; with a limp white shift hanging from her shoulders, she looked almost Hindu. Something about her nose was deeply disturbing, as if it had been bought at a no-exchanges-no-return sale at Macy's but when taken home had proven a size too small. In contrast to the hostility that greeted my colleagues on earlier visits, I was barely acknowledged. Perhaps by this time they realized that insurance adjusters weren't to be trusted but were otherwise harmless. The mother stood over an open grill, cooking hamburger. Miscalculating their mealtime was annoying. Dinner might serve to distract them from the force of my argument.

The girl looked at me vacantly from behind her bandaged leg, propped up on a plastic-thatched beach chair. "Ralph will be out in a minute," her mother said. "He just got in from the city." I sat on the bench of the picnic table and tried unsuccessfully to make talk about the humidity. The girl said nothing. Even if she'd had two good legs, I would have marked her down as a terminal case.

When Ralph appeared, I found it difficult to believe he was the wild man who had threatened Shelly and chased Shields with a badminton racket. He wore black pleated trousers and an undershirt, stiff hairs poked out from under his arms, and he was tiny, even shorter than his wife. He took his hands from his pants pockets, opened two beers, stuck one in front of me and began a careful study of the label.

"How'd it go?" his wife wanted to know. She turned the meat, pressing the patties down with a spatula, sending sparks up from the coals.

"A crummy week. All the buyers are on vacation." He looked at me. "I sell knitting machines, but nobody is around in August. It's a dying business, anyway. The Japs do it cheaper."

"Did you speak to Billie?"

"Let's not go into that. She wants me to get a loan from her brother, but I'm not that hard up yet. You know how it is with family."

"Stupid pride." This was said to the girl, but the sound easily carried to the table.

"I'll 'stupid pride' you. Come on back to the city and you'll see what it takes in this heat. Listen, fella, your company or association or whatever it is has been out here before and we couldn't work anything out, so I'm gonna see a lawyer. There's nothing more to say."

"Well, Mr. Kovicki, we want to make sure before you go to the expense and trouble of a lawyer and have to wait all those years before this thing is settled—we want to give it one more chance to see there's a place where the minds can meet."

Ralph dipped into his cooler and passed over another can of beer.

"How much do you feel is fair? That might be a basis for discussion. We aren't as hard-hearted as you may think. And if some ready cash might help, well..."

"But you'll cheat me. Look, I work like a son of a bitch all week and don't bring home enough to scrape by. That's a fact. You make me an offer and I might take it. This girl of mine is hurt real bad. If she limps in five years, she should have something to show for it. I really don't want you to offer me *anything*—I might take it."

"Mr. Kovicki, if you think any settlement we would make might be unfair, you are free to check with—"

"You're sounding stupid again, Ralph."

This time there was no stage whisper, and suddenly his rage was out front. He ran at his wife, pushing her back from the grill, palms jostling her shoulders. He pushed, then lowered his hands, following her as she stumbled back.

The girl struggled to her feet, hobbling toward them. "Papa, stop." She grabbed her father around the waist, keeping him away, her face in the small of his back. "Papa, stop it."

After he'd shaken her off, Ralph turned on me. "You bastard. Why should you care what the company has to pay for this? All I want is a fair shake. Look at this kid. She can hardly walk."

I was too well trained to get involved. During the rage I played Mr. Cool, just sitting on the bench, not rising to his insult. Let him blow. But the worm of defeat gnawed anyway: I wanted to settle this case, and Ralph didn't; he was willing to let it destruct.

He returned to his beer, and mother and daughter retreated with the meat to the cabin.

"This is such a crock."

We sat.

"Listen, pal, make me an offer. No, I take that back. Don't."

"Well, Mr. Kovicki, I think with the bills and all the trouble you've had that seven hundred fifty would be justifiable in this case."

I surprised myself by making the first offer, but I wanted to find out where he stood. It seemed an acceptable risk. Besides, the smell of a cage had begun to get to me, and I wanted to leave as soon as possible. What the hell, if I settled for double my first offer, I would still have closed a case no one else could touch for a bargain price.

Ralph didn't reply. We stayed at the picnic table until the mosquitoes grew fierce, and then he motioned me into the cabin. Two squares connected by a cooking alcove, chipped planking, torn screens. In the far room mother and daughter watched a television variety show, the tube throwing its gray light into the front room. The volume was turned low, giving a muffled roar to the sound-track laughter that drifted in to where we sat. Ralph went to the fridge, but this time I declined; I was beginning to feel awash in foam.

"Tell me how you get to seven fifty, because I figure it differently."

Here was an opportunity to turn it around, to take his request and turn it into a question. But I muffed it. With hindsight I can see that I had already lost. Professional negotiators will tell you that differences in quantity are difficult to defend; it is differences in principle that stick. Tasting a settlement, I was driven until my back nearly touched the wall. The seven fifty crumbled to a thousand, slipped to twelve fifty and then fifteen hundred. I had run through the end of my own rationalizations.

At that point I stiffened. The women lay motionless in the other room, as if the same hand that had turned off the television had put them to sleep. The mother curled around a pillow, but the girl looked like a corpse, her bad leg pointing an accusing toe in my direction. Suddenly, I understood the nose. They had taken her to a butcher, and he had botched the job. It hadn't worked out at all.

Hunched over his beer can, Ralph opened and closed his mouth but said nothing. His chest heaved, air hissed from his nose, but he remained mute.

I tried to concentrate on the cicadas. Why did they make that sound? Was it a mating call or a note of contented feeding? Did they do it because they wanted to or did it just happen?

By midnight I had been driven to seventeen fifty, but I still might have salvaged pride and been able to return to Arnold with my head not sticking out from between my legs if I had been less impatient, more resistant to the gambler's call to throw it all on one horse and be done with it. I might even have gotten away unscathed if I had found the strength to urinate, but for some reason I couldn't, not in that house. Which is why they pay veterans more than rookies—not because they're smarter, but because they're more patient and will relieve a bursting bladder anywhere they find a can.

Amateur that I was, I tried to recoup all with a big bet. I looked at my watch and tried to act tough.

"We've gone on long enough, Ralph. They don't pay me for overtime. I have to leave in twenty minutes. After that, I can't offer you anything. If you want two thousand, I'll go for it, but it's got to be now. Otherwise, my offer goes down a hundred a minute until it and me are gone. You hear me?"

I knew it was a blunder the minute the words were out of my mouth, but out they had come. All my planning hadn't stopped them. The only question was whether Ralph, slumping in his chair, hands folded in his lap, studying the room's disarray as if it were a blackboard covered by mathematical formuli, had grasped that I had made the supreme error of threatening something I couldn't bring myself to do. A negotiator without commitment to his threats or promises will be worn down by even a thoughtless adversary. He has lost, paying in humiliation for a moment's impatient bravado.

The rest is a blur. Sometime later Ralph dozed off. I had to rouse him, squatting on the floor, my hand patting his knee. I whispered, not because of the sleeping women but so that Arnold wouldn't hear.

"Look, let's wrap this up. I'll give you thirty-five hundred. I can't go much higher. Here are the forms. Sign on the bottom and let me out of here."

Ralph sighed, and for the first time in six hours his face showed something other than anger or sadness, though joy it wasn't. He raised his brows, shook his head in an effort to remember the forgotten evening and took the papers to a small table. He was about to sign when he hesitated.

"What about the five dollars and ninety-eight cents?"

"What's that?"

"My out-of-pocket for the bandage."

"Oh yeah, make it an even thirty-six. Anything."

I handed him the check and ran shivering to my car.

Arnold was kind. Outraged, disbelieving, but ultimately, in his schoolmasterish way, kind. He explained that I had met Br'er Rabbit, the laconic hare who persuaded his captors that his heart's desire was to be thrown into the brier patch, a wish they maliciously denied him. Ralph had so masked his true feelings that to this day I don't know if he felt I had strong-armed him into an unfair settlement or whether, as Arnold said, the whole minuet was a carefully laid trap, a production worthy of Stanislavsky. From that day on I stopped checking the score sheets. Fair-haired boy no more.

At least I'd had a lesson. After the first wave of defeat-induced nausea passed over—leaving me breathless and creaky for days—I convinced myself that Ralph had served an educational purpose. Of course, my self-improvement was hampered by not being able to articulate what this purpose was. However, there must be some chestnut of wisdom to extract from the experience; otherwise, I would have to mark myself down as a failure.

Pulling in my head, I saw as few claimants as possible, and even with those, dealt cautiously by refusing to settle unless they insisted. I took smirks of toothy pleasure from supercilious colleagues, especially Shields, and an excessive number of "Buck ups" from Arnold. If I could just boil down the lesson into a little fortune-cookie message, I could regroup my forces. Instead of "Buck up" I wanted to hear Arnold say, "That kid just keeps coming. You can't keep a real pro down."

As others began to label me depressed, I realized they might be right. My search turned frantic. I explored several hypotheses: winning and losing is a false dichotomy; cooperation advances our interests as much as competition; manipulation is never absent from human affairs. Anything that would help me smother the memory. But while I found evidence in what had happened supporting all these principles, statements of objective truth didn't work. Apparently I had to write my own fortune.

Shelly came to my rescue. We were sitting in our usual clubhouse box waiting for the feature race. I hadn't looked up from my program all evening.

"What animal you feel like?"

"What do you mean?"

"Don't play dumb. When I wait a month for them to slip a classy horse in with groaners and he goes off at ten to one and at the last minute I persuade myself that he can't do it so bet the favorite and then the one I've been waiting for laps the field, I feel like a pig. Oink, oink."

"A turkey."

"Good. On your feet. Chest out, stomach in. Now, here in front of the assembled, your peer group for the evening: Gobble, gobble."

"Really?"

"Yes."

"Gobble, gobble."

"Stop whispering."

"Gobble, gobble."

"Better. See the permanent wave of red hair surrounding that yak-yak mouth over there to the left? Make her turn around."

"Gobble."

"Gobble, gobble."

"Gobble, gobble, gob-ble, gob-ble. GOBBLE."

"Excellent. Now you feel stupid. It's over. You have nothing to avoid. We can talk about this race."

Teddy is in his horse phase. It used to be underwater photography; before fish, it was blackjack counting systems; before that, magic. Teddy has an OTB credit card, a secret number, a dial-a-bet code name, and a library of crafty be-smart-and-win-at-the-track books whose authors all claim to have retired to Santa Barbara. Like many lawyers, he loves puzzles. In the winter he studies old racing forms and ponders game theory. Both his work and the ponies engage him in the infinite demands of mastering an infinite number of systems. Effortlessly, his mind moves from documenting the byzantine ways U.S. Steel keeps a lid on its black workers to calculating the average speed of four-year-old geldings for six furlongs over the Belmont main track.

Early in spring I call to set up our annual pilgrimage. Teddy is off in Denver or Atlanta, showing some reluctant federal judge that the local school board is still building new schools in places where whites will never go. The civil-rights movement is just an echo for most of us, but not for Teddy. On an easel he'll fix a map of the city and stand with a pointer while his gofer flips plastic overlays. Poster-paint blues and reds show where the races live; shaded squares mark each school put up in the last decade, always placed deep inside a blue or red area rather than on a border between the two.

The superintendent squirms and huddles with his lawyer. Teddy calls his experts to the stand. They testify about the maps, explain the demographics, the principles of site selection and pupil assignment, the interplay of housing patterns and district lines, how many buses the district bought before blacks wanted to ride them to white schools. The board lawyer grumbles: "Everyone knows parent income assigns kids to school. Race doesn't enter in." Teddy evokes the Fourteenth Amendment. The judge retires, and Teddy looks at his watch. "I wonder who won the feature at Aqueduct."

Teddy is passionate about his work wherever he finds it, and he likes obstacles. When outrage fails, he summons craft. He has stayed with cases that I now avoid. One reason is that his father taught him how. For Teddy, a trip to court is like playing catch or carving model planes, an afternoon with Dad. Another reason is that he resists generalization. Like a horse race, a case is a clash of particulars, never repeated. I lost interest when the issues turned from removing barriers to forcing access. My loathing for public school made me a poor lawyer for those seeking to enter one.

On a sweet day in April, the kind that makes me sure I live in New York for the women on the street, I pick Teddy up in midtown in front of the stone slab where I worked for ten years. An architect friend joked about this structure: "I have my office there so I don't have to look at it." We creep crosstown and wiggle onto the Expressway. Teddy steadies papers on his briefcase and reads the latest word from the Supremes, some jargon that rejects some other jargon—in this instance, unfortunately, the latter a principle that the civil-rightsers won in the court below.

"A little joy from the Justices," Teddy says. "Henceforth and hereafter we will have to prove a *purpose* to discriminate; it is not enough to show a disproportionate, adverse impact on blacks. We have to come up with an invidious mental state, evidence of what is going on in someone's head when they pluck names from a list."

"Oh shit, what will the Court do next?"

We frown with disapproval, bonded by commiseration. The Court is like an old friend, not very reliable but occasionally courageous, who has started showing up drunk at dinner parties. In the silence that follows I know from having carried a briefcase with this man through a hundred swinging courtroom doors that both of us are groping for something that will excuse the most high, for a justification of the rule or at least some evidence of bad lawyering to explain its announcement in this case. Our first impulse is to find a sensible and consistent thread to this lunacy, even though it has been thrown in our teeth.

Once you get the habit, the lawyer's claw grips tight and deep; it takes years to dislodge. Oblivious of the snarling traffic and the day of pleasure ahead, we sort out potential allowances. The view is different from the top of the pyramid; it is easier to talk about justice than to deliver it, and so on. We start with the assumed rationality of the Supremes just as we would assume—if we believed in one—that there was method to even the wildest caprice of a Supreme Being. Though for me the grip has been loosening lately; I was moving away before Slade's call turned me back.

It took only the interval between one parkway exit and the next to conclude that the Justices expected technology to step into the breach: industry would develop a bigot detector that rivaled the polygraph. A Geiger counter for bad intentions. When it comes to pigeonholing the unknowable, it helps to be a lawyer. How did I ever get into this business?

The track is in sight. I shift gears in Teddy's fancy sports car.

"There's a real standout on this card, a grass horse that wins half its races."

We pull into the clubhouse lot, buy ham on rye so stale it chips molars, and settle into the thin weekday crowd.

Teddy reads out his speed ratings, the class differential co-efficient, the percentage each horse is in the money. To humor him I write down the numbers. He whips out a slide-rule calculator and presses the keys like a typist gone mad.

Ishmael Santiago. Teddy, stop your data processing and look here. There's a Santiago shipper from Bowie in this race." I'm surprised at the high pitch to my voice; heads turn, all eager for a tip. "Only raced four times and never better than sixth. Last time out he was outrun by seventeen lengths. This is for me."

"First it's a her and second you're crazy. She only rates a forty-six against thirty-five-hundred-dollar platers. Now, look at the three horse. Breaks fast, drops back and comes on again. Claimed by a good barn in March. Hasn't won since. Cordero's the jock."

We wander down to the paddock and sit on the grass. Honchita's jockey is wearing cerise; her weather-faced trainer squints at the sun as he lifts the saddle. Derisively, Teddy notes the kidney sweat streaming down her legs. The tote board flickers; the odds drop to 8-1. That does it. As the bugle blows the horses onto the track, I put my arm around Teddy's shoulder and steer him to the betting windows.

"When I was thirteen, my father took me to the old Belmont, up on the roof where he could get a tan while he handicapped. He opened his scratch sheet and started chuckling, a big mysterious smile covering his face. He lectured: 'Well, boy, here is a lesson. There are horses that are known as shippers. Trainers run them into shape at Booneville Downs, truck them east to stick on real money where it won't be noticed, put a sharp jockey in the stirrups, and the horse scores wire to wire. This fellow Santiago'—and now he's whispering—'he does it all the time. Usually, he puts the shipper in a race following a hundred-thousand-dollars-added stake. All the horses in that one are sired by bluebloods. The social register is attending. The crowd is distracted by television. The track presents the winning owner's wife with a silver platter. While the bettors gawk, the next race goes off and Santiago's anonymous gelding laps the field. I've brought you out here so you won't have to learn these things the hard way.'"

But Teddy doesn't hear. He's correlating number three's speed differential with the dead-weight factor. I bet Honchita to win. By the time we find our seats, the odds are down to 6-1. I pick up Teddy's *Supreme Court Reporter* and read another horror from the Burger Court until he puts down his glasses.

"Well, you warned me," he says, "but a forty-six at Bowie. Who do you think your father likes in the next race?"

Eight months before I am born my grandmother is in the hospital, dying of cancer. Her doctor comes in to take his daily look at life slipping away, sees a young couple visiting and notices a lump on the neck of the curly-headed fellow standing by the bed.

"Had any trouble with that?" he asks, motioning to what my father thinks is a boil.

"Tight shirt collars," my father says. He pulls at the white oxford. "Have to buy a bigger size."

"Better have that looked at, young man." And he is gone.

Of course, my mother insists. A week later she is summoned to one of those brownstones in the East Seventies where New Yorkers keep their doctors. The old man with red mustache and oversized freckles has treated her parents since before the trucking business went bust. But he barely knows my mother, and probably thinks of her as the child in her father's wallet. Hands jammed in the patch pockets of his white coat, he tries to be matter-of-fact.

"Well, it's Hodgkin's."

She turns the word over in her mind and comes up with nothing. In the city you hear the traffic only when everything is quiet, a rarity. Otherwise it becomes a part of you, an ever-present inner noise to be dismissed.

"Sometimes it takes five years. We don't know much about it."

"For what?"

The doctor is plainly annoyed. "Come back in a week, and we'll talk about what to do." My mother doesn't get up until he says, "What do you want me to do, cry?"

Later she finds a book. *A usually chronic, advancing, ultimately fatal disease of unknown etiology, manifested by progressive enlargement of the lymph nodes and frequently of the spleen and liver.* She goes to the dingy apartment on upper Broadway and makes her pact with the devil, a hand-on-the-belly vow, never to tell. She was a pampered daughter. Her father sent his trucks around town, but his heart wasn't in it. A reader, a great reader, was the kindest thing his in-laws could say. Her mother was the tough one. She quit her job as a private eye for the Fifth Avenue Coach Company to keep the business going. Her forte was to catch malingerers by playing social worker. Talking her way into the houses of employees claiming on-the-job injury, she found broken legs that were actually sprains, drivers on sick leave working down at the docks. My mother was a second daughter, whose sister abdicated her responsibility to overachieve, leaving the task of holding up the family colors to the younger child. She had to marry to grow up. Now, to prove it, she would keep the news to herself. We'll see what those doctors know. It turned out they were right about the disease but blew the prognosis. He lived twenty years, giving me an opportunity to get in on the action.

It is no secret that people experience time differently. The Hungarian refugee dandy who taught me international politics sauntered into his classroom as if arriving at his favorite café for an after-work Campari. For the same reason that Rudy is always five minutes early, Clare is always five minutes late. My friend Binni has patients who don't understand the fifty-minute hour. My timing now is unpredictable, but in those days I was on an express. Whoosh out of the city to the five-thousand-dollar toy house on the toy lawn in Queens bought because the only older person my mother knew who looked like she'd make it to spring, a real-estate broker, lived around the corner. Whoosh off the breast, onto the potty and forward march to the Ivy League.

It's parents' night at private school, and my wife Connie is distressed. The first of Dee's teachers, Mr. McGill, is a sweety, but one of the fathers, dapper in a sharkskin suit, rises to ask whether McGill really believes that learning can be fun.

While McGill tries to swallow that one, Connie mutters: "Obviously this is a school for the children of strivers." We cross a hallway to the math room, where we are confronted with Monotone Maury, number one on my daughter's hit list: "In addition, there are problems working with the parallelogram, the rhomboid and the rectangle—culminating, of course, in the circle. Very important, the circle. The children will progress to placement of rhomboids inside of circles and circles inside of rhomboids. We want them to think. This is a thinking world."

The science instructor has an entertaining face, but she talks only grades. "Now, this workbook is a reinforcement tool. Our tests are motivators. We specialize in short answers on our tests because the SAT's emphasize short answers." Now we're down to basics, no glib parental rejoinders here. I try to be philosophic: one teacher a year isn't so bad; I can only think of three or four good ones in eighteen years of sitting at desks. Dee is too hardy a city weed to be damaged by anything said in a classroom. But Connie is seething. By virtue of old money, she had it different. The South Side of Chicago was one of the nation's great storehouses of university brats. In the ninth grade she was given an A in biology for writing a hundred rhymed couplets about a mythical microorganism of her own creation named the Pebamia. She can still recognize false Solomon's seal at a hundred paces. But I loathe Chicago despite the glory of her education. First there were the pitchers in the Cubs' Ebbets Field bullpen who told me to fuck off when I stuck out a program and a pen; then Mayor Daley's judges, crude bastards, one of whom tried to mousetrap me into suborning perjury. Chicago organizes the chaos that New York lets take its course.

In the cafeteria the headmaster congratulates us on our children and says that student test scores are up to a 670 average. Dee is proud of her school and would resent our doubts. My own high school friends were hardly contemplative; they could all compute their grade average to four decimal places. If I didn't go that route, it was only because I was never good at math. To her despair, Connie is unemployed.

The United States has been engaged in shooting wars for virtually half my lifetime, but I have never seen a drop of blood. The Second World War, the war of childhood, retains a special place in my heart. We were surrounded by it. Despite the miles of barbed wire on the beaches, cannon barrels sticking out from the eelgrass, bunkers dug in the dunes, our war never quite fit with the grainy newsreel artillery barrages, the turds dropped on Axis industry from the open maws of B-17's. Planes roared in and out of the airfield across the Bay—Grumman Hellcats, Lockheed F-47's, Lightnings. Bubble gum cards came to life. I learned to distinguish the make from the roar of the engines. I collected newspapers and coffee cans filled with fat. My mother delivered sandwiches to the bunkers in a wooden station wagon, the kind that astonished Dee once at a country fair—"Look, Mom," she said, "a half-timbered station wagon." We had an air-raid helmet and a government-issue flashlight. When eventually my father was called for a physical, my mother rushed to the draft board with a file of letters from the doctors. Back came a 4-F.

"Why?"

"Don't question your luck, Jed... Maybe your anemia?"

Fortunately for her, my father's anemia meant blood transfusions, and ultimately he picked up a case of jaundice. Now, here was something she could talk about. "It's your jaundice that makes you tired." "Be careful, remember your jaundice." He withered, bald at twenty-eight. Old daddy, young mommy, little hero waiting for his chance.

I remember that I longed to have the house to myself, to move the problem elsewhere. Whatever my dim understanding of the medical situation,

I sensed there was a weakness akin to the symptoms of old age. Since it tempted me to revolution, this weakness was despised. I had to take it into account, I couldn't push because he might topple, and I didn't want responsibility for the collapse. For self-protection, I began to look out for him. A reluctance to do anything that might affect his health kept me in line. A showy stability—a prematurity, if you will—has stuck with me ever since, plagued me not only with a conscience that I have often wished away, but with a need that others recognize I have one. As with so many of my colleagues, the lawyer in me emerged long before I started making vocational choices. Its first task was the organization of my own defense. "No wonder," Connie says, in her I've-got-your-number way, "you relish your children's mistakes."

I've maintained the predictable amnesia about my mother's role during these years, but she must have been an unusually virtuous woman. The blond-haired resident doctor with the Southern accent who some years later tended my father during the last gasps of Hodgkin's, jaundice, amyloidosis and surgical incompetence was attracted to her before the funeral. She wiped it out of her mind, accustomed to that sort of thing. On her first date, a year later, she looked well-preserved and inexperienced. I waited up; I couldn't fall asleep until I heard her key in the lock.

Once I brought the autopsy to my analyst, Manny. Even he gasped (you get ten points for a shrink's gasp). My father was a walking edition of the *Merck's Manual*.

He was uncertain, knew and didn't know, had no name for his premonition. After many years of believing in the right to know, I have concluded that my mother was correct to leave him in ignorance. Had he understood the odds against him, he'd have spent all those years in bed. Power is reserved to those who believe they can exercise it—or is gathered by those able to show it. Rudy and I have devised a negotiating game for our students. We divide them in pairs. As in duplicate bridge, a member of each pair plays the same hand. We send them out for two weeks: settle the dispute or fail the course. On a chart we rank the settlements. Bright women do poorly; their clients are taken to the cleaners. Self-confident, vain men are easy winners. In a sinister mood I match the best of the sexes. The man will break off negotiations, storm out of the room, use his body as a weapon, threaten, cajole and, most effective of all, insinuate. The woman will be a superior writer, sharper analyst, better person. She will know the power in her position, but when it comes to showing it, making it live, she is still learning. On the way up she is betrayed by the subjective. If she learns the lesson, I will be thanked for what makes me guilty.

When I needed a vacation from responsibility for my father's problems, I had a handy and deserving scapegoat in his employers—the firm of Jones and Chively, or, as my parents in fear and awe referred to it, The Company. Located in a Midwestern city where it snowed from October to May, The Company was run by Sebastian Conte. Around our house he was always called King Conte, even though the idea for the business had come to him while he was in prison. He was doing a stretch in Leavenworth for mail fraud and shared a cell with a tax evader named Wentworth Chively. Jones was the factor who bankrolled them later. He got his name on the letter-head but never made it into our Iliad.

Conte and Chively were both chiselers with strong antisocial tenden-cies. In prison they became fast friends, drank smuggled bourbon, hoarded scrip, protected each other from more physical cons. They sat up summer nights plotting vast consumer frauds. Chively was irrepressible; prison sharpened his appetite for the world of business. He was up at six, before the trustees blew the morning whistle, chinning on the bars, counting deep knee bends and situps. In the gloomy prison dawn he would bellow, "It's a great day for the race!" Conte, leaning on his elbow, remaining on his cot until the last possible moment, learned his part. Small and dusky, with a thin nose much too big for his face, his secret power over people, and the source of their distrust, was that his physique perfectly embodied conspir-acy. His ears suggested clandestine conversation, his mouth revenge, his eyes vendetta. The judge slapped Conte with a two-year sentence because he had the appearance of a habitual criminal. It was a view played back to him often, but he never understood; he thought, I only wanted to make money like the rest.

"What race?"

Chively would thump his chest. "The human race."

The morning ritual included marking a big X in red pencil on the cell calendar. There were block letters in boxes for each date beneath E. F. NE-SMITH, General Insurance, Kansas City. Methodically, Chively filled in the segments, obscuring the dates. The two men became lovers: the son of an Indianapolis haberdasher and a balding ex-accountant of whom the govern-ment had made an example to show the federal tax laws meant business. Neither had anything to do with men before or would again. They had no problem adjusting but kept it secret. It was part of the prison routine, like swallowing greasy soup and cold potatoes—necessary for survival. They were partners, went everywhere together. Sometimes they dug ditches, sometimes fitted tubing in the prison shop. All through the humid Kansas summer Sebastian Conte watched Wentworth Chively cross days off the calendar. In the fall Chively was paroled and Conte had to share the cell with a half-Indian hijacker from Dakota.

The million-dollar idea came to Conte one morning as he stood at the sink sloshing water over his body. He tore the month of October off the calendar, folded it in neat squares and stuck it under the mattress with his canteen chits. Not only calendars but playing cards, ashtrays, ballpoints, metal pencils, desk sets, butane lighters, telephone dialers, corkscrews, steak knives, ice buckets. Items, the King called them; not tape measures, cigarette boxes or key cases, but items. A new item for the line. All you do is click this, cock that, and it pours, lights, pushes, pulls, twists, wiggles like a reptile. Sell them not to consumers but to business for use as giveaways. As a child, I could never make them work. No matter what I stole from my father's sample case to show off at school, the lead broke, the clocks stopped ticking, the cards lacked an ace. God's will, no doubt. In those days people actually frightened their children with hell. When I try to fathom Dee's immediate and unafraid apprehension of reality, I have to remember that for her hell is an expletive, not a place. No one has ever claimed she killed Christ.

In the late sixties everyone at Good Works—then my place of employment—debated what we called "whether things have really changed." Veteran members of the staff were certain that conditions had improved; the younger lawyers dissented. The division crossed racial lines. "Never forget," my boss told me, "Thurgood Marshall slept at a Jim Crow hotel the night before he argued *Brown v. Board of Education* to the Supreme Court." It embarrassed me that I sided with the older generation only because it had been fifteen years since anyone called me a Christ killer.

I still keep a desk at Good Works—less from conviction than to be near my friend Annie. I spend most of my time now at the law school where I teach a few courses and, with Rudy and Clare, supervising students at a clinic on the edge of Harlem. Our boss leaves us alone because he's smart enough to know we will do his bidding only if no one tries to instruct us how. I call him the Soft Killer. He gets his way by deference and by going with the punches—but he gets his way.

I have three offices in all and spend part of every day at each. A woman called recently trying to sell me a subscription to *The Wall Street Journal*. I couldn't get her to stop talking. She said she was so happy to have reached me, that I had more phone numbers than her bookmaker.

"You don't sell the item," my father would say, "you sell the package, the man's name, the company logo, the girl's tits. The art of selling is you have a dilapidated house, the roof leaks, the walls need plastering, the pump backs up, the furnace turns off in an ice storm, but out front is a towering umbrella elm. Only tree like it for miles. All summer long it gives off enough shade for three picnics. You can hang a swing from the lower branches or climb sixty feet straight up. Room for a treehouse. You sell this house for the tree. You get an outrageous price because of the tree. No lies, son. No need to exaggerate, cajole, mislead. Never oversell. Just find the tree and sell it. The tree gives the buyer comfort, like the chrome gismo on a Cadillac."

Well, he made money selling trees, not big money but enough to help him forget the Depression. His routine in those days started with a good puke. After a big breakfast, his best meal, of sunnyside eggs, crisp bacon, buttered toast, black coffee, he wandered upstairs to throw up, brush his teeth, pack a briefcase, smile to one and all, kiss mother and son goodbye, and off to the train station. Me stirring cornflakes, she staring out the window, until the twin gut noises—first from him, then the plumbing—subsided in memory, signaling that we could relax. Another day in suburbia.

He walked to the Long Island Railroad and eased into a seat in the card car to wait for his commuter cronies. Hollywood gin, bridge, even hearts. In lean weeks he fed his family and his bookmaker's family from this game. In a drawer there was a black suede cigarette case with gold-plated initials. How much, I wonder, did you have to lose to get Christmas presents from your bookie?

From Penn Station he went to his office, where he packed the day's samples, picked up a pad of order blanks and checked his pen. A neat order pad and a working pen were absolutely essential when closing in for the kill. A few appointments made by phone to make sure no one thought he jobbed sundries, and out into the clotted Manhattan streets. Then he had to deal with the gatekeepers. The bosses were surrounded by receptionists, brothers-in-law, foremen. Sometimes brazen, sometimes obsequious, my father slipped through to shadow the top man as he swaggered around the factory, aiming his message at a moving target. They ignored him, but he kept talking. When they said no, he perked up. "A man who says no has a reason; if you're any good, you have a better one." He winked Jewish to the Russians and Poles, old New York to the Episcopalians; talked Notre Dame football scores to the Irish. He honed the patter, practiced his timing. Learned when to flash the gadgetry. "In every line there is a fondler. You may want to sell a Rockwell calendar, but first you show the fondler."

Men leaning over yards of fabric in gray lofts, looking too clever to be sold, studying patterns under fluorescent light. On he spieled. "You have to have your name in front of them; if they don't know your name, you're nothing."

"Listen, mister, they all know my name. Sometimes that's the trouble."

"Call me Jed," my father said gaily. "Rhymes with bed." Human contact gave him second wind. "You work with buyers. What the hell good is a bottle of booze at Christmas time? It's done by New Year's. Now, this desk diary with an imprint of Rubenstein Fabrics—Laces, Brocades, Woolens, To the Trade—sits on a desk all year long. Three hundred and sixty-five messages." The boss frowned at his cutters, tried to work free. "One more thing and I'm going. Give me one minute of your time by the clock. Then I'm out. Sixty seconds and you go back to your supervising."

Gently he rested a hand on the man's shoulders, steered him to a cutting table, brushed aside shreds of gabardine, placed his watch on the table. "One minute." He pointed to the pulsing hand. "You count." Next an order blank with an X by the signature line and an uncapped fountain pen. "Okay, here goes and I'm out. You have to give them gifts. That's the system. No, don't interrupt. This is my minute. I'm here to serve you, but if you don't need what I have to sell, you shouldn't have it. You have to give them gifts. Five hundred diaries will run you four and a quarter apiece, boxed and ready for mailing. On the desk all year long. Company name, phone, address, a few words about the business, maybe 'All languages perfectly spoken.' Whiskey will cost you a buck more, and they'll never remember who gave it to them. Pick up the pen if you want; don't if you don't. One minute, see, as good as my word."

Then he shut up, fumbled with his sample case, offered no resistance. Only with the silence did the customer hear the logic. He had to buy something. You gave liquor to the schwartze elevator man. The books had a certain substance, and in the wings earnest Jed was right there to serve. Of course, the customer signed and the next year ordered by phone—two hundred fifty more and a couple hundred butane lighters besides. It was simple except for Jed's gut. But he'd puke the next morning and make everything right.

He graduated from this to Fortune 500 blockbuster deals with executives whose yes could make him six months' salary in an afternoon. The fondlers had to be imports. A minute with an order blank and a pen didn't work here. In these meetings with advertising managers and vice presidents sitting around oiled-walnut conference tables, he was never Jewish. He bought them lunches he couldn't afford, haunted Park Avenue office buildings, carrying his deal to marketing, purchasing, finance and personnel. There were sales that collapsed after months of trotting up and down the organization chart. There were chiselers looking for kickbacks. He was cooled out by receptionists and often went two months without a sale, but the size of his commission made it worthwhile. Then with a Norman Rockwell calendar he cracked an oil company. Its picture said, "Your friendly neighborhood service station descends from the village smithy."

He began to spend more time in his office on the phone, less on the subway. He was assigned his own secretary; her name came up in every conversation. "I'll have Lila do it." "Ask Lila to check my book." He opened an account with a broker. His ties came from Sulka's. On Friday afternoons he still slipped off to the track, but now he was betting with abandon at the fifty-dollar window. Perhaps he needed to raise the stakes to the point where the next race mattered—then there would be a next race.

A vice president flew east to tell him King Conte was impressed with his sales record. On the spot he was promoted to district manager. "The salary will be less," he told my mother, "but there'll be a regular paycheck, no more hunting for commissions." A manager is a leader of men; he must make them produce. A coach of quotas.

It was the beginning of the end. In the modern corporation, managers don't do anything specific. In economic terms their function has never been justified. Reputable scholars have published lengthy articles in learned journals hypothesizing that management makes its own work. Compared to the pinstripers who run the big babies, Pirandello was an amateur, academic hustlers belong in the minors, Harry Houdini was an illusionist fit only for the bar mitzvah circuit. In Jed's case living suddenly seemed less of a necessity.

But he took the job anyway—took it as proof that they loved him, though the only sign was that they sent him to the Midwestern city where it always snowed for conventions and sales meetings. Despite top-heavy hostesses parading the new line and demos of the latest ruthless closing technique, they mostly played cards. The politics of the company was decided over the poker table by shirt-sleeved men sipping rye. He won so much that they had to take notice: "Wouldja believe, the only Jew in the company is a card shark."

One winter he rode to Chicago with Barnett, the vice president for the entire Northeast region. Stuck in a blizzard between Buffalo and Cleveland, they played hand after hand of Hollywood gin, Jed's idea of heaven. The heat went off, ice formed in their water glasses, but he didn't notice. Eventually, Barnett revealed how he and Sharkey of the Kansas City office were grooming their man to take over when Conte retired; that Conte was talking merger, a big boost for the stock. By Detroit, Jed was ahead seventeen hundred dollars.

Barnett owned a cattle ranch in Wyoming, a tax shelter, bought after the King invested in a similar operation in Texas. No wonder the calendar artists had been switched to Western motifs: open-vested cowgirls teasing broncos, wrestling steers, nakedly frolicking in haylofts. Cattle with Conte's brand. Samples had the King himself astride a yellow palomino, Captain Hook on a horse. "He buys a ranch," Barnett explained. "I buy a ranch. We talk ranches." Jed was dazzled but could only talk about me.

"We can use him out there some summer," Barnett said. "Make a man out of him. Shovel shit, learn the stock."

Jed promptly blew a hand. "You really think that might be possible?"

The more Barnett lost, the more highly he thought of Jed. By Chicago, Jed was the man to run the whole New York operation. "You know the territory. I'll see what I can do, but there are these creeps who golf with the Old Man. Never sold a keycase, all they do is set quotas. But I'll try. Deal."

The thread of Jed's life frayed at the point where his official position was to take care of others. He had just so much strength; there was not enough to spread around. Nor was he helped by the war between sales force and executives, a class struggle as bitter as any found in *Das Kapital*. The front office bitched about the men in the field, and the salesmen screamed that their orders were screwed up at the factory. What good were Christmas gifts that arrived in February?

To Jed's amazement Barnett was canned and a potbellied Captain Queeg type was brought in from Toledo to toughen up the division. Jed's style of leadership was a soft-spoken one-on-one: sympathy, gentle encouragement, how's the missus and kids. Queeg could have led the Green Bay Packers. He harassed his managers, doubled the quotas, posted wall-size graphs covered with red ink showing the gap between performance and potential. Jed was ordered to get rid of the deadwood: "Take this Mancini. Hasn't earned enough in the last three months to pay for his memo pads."

"Now, Bill, Mancini is coming along. Only a year out of a cab, he's making inroads in the Italian community. Got a problem with getting in the door. We have to give him some time to develop."

But Queeg played rough. "You aren't tough enough, Jed. You're an idealist."

The worst, of course, was that secretly Jed thought Queeg was right. Contrary to popular belief, he had told me, the most effective commercials were not the imaginative, the prizewinners, but the most obnoxious. For the best results give the public two minutes of the company name, preferably screeched two octaves above middle C by a raucous Jezebel. And he no longer believed he could make it on the outside. A prisoner of his papers, pushing figures into the out box, he began to do Queeg's bidding—choosing one slow-motion death for another. Before they hauled him to the hospital suffering from anorexia, nausea and vomiting, the ambulance attendant carefully noting "White male, pale, apprehensive, confused, in acute distress, his skin cool and clammy," he'd even given up going to the track.

In *Sahara* Bogey and a few resourceful tankers defeated half the German army. Hiding in the dunes, they routed Rommel and his legions. Begged by my mother to taste the faith of my forefathers, like lima beans, at the age of nine I put it to the pudding-faced Reform rabbi who looked as if he shaved with a bread knife: "Am I as holy, as close to God, with Humphrey in the desert as in your temple?"

He was outraged. We were nothing to write the seminary about, the congregation small and miserly, the house of worship little more than a converted gazebo dwarfed by the spire of St. Francis de Sales. The bug eyes my question evoked may simply have reflected that the rabbi couldn't distinguish me from my evil Purim pageant Haman, but his answer rang totally false. Except for once it was definitive. No parable from the Apochrypha, no anecdotes from the *shtetl*. I must have touched a nerve.

Because we go away on weekends, Dee doesn't even know she has the opportunity to reject the limas. In all fairness, though, I must admit that the indifference passed on to her could not have been produced only by a callow rabbi's failure to measure up to the great Hillel. In my parent's bedside table I had early discovered the confusion that is Mary Baker Eddy. I have nothing against Christian Science; in fact, one must be rather fond of a denomination that has felt the call to populate the world with quiet places to read and meditate. But whatever the sect's allure to the sick, and it may be considerable, its holy books speak only muddle to a son hoping to gather in his father's spirit without drinking his blood. "A patient's belief is more or less formed by his doctor's belief in the case, even though the doctor says nothing to support his theory. His thoughts and his patient's commingle, and the stronger rule the weaker. Hence the importance that doctors be Christian Scientists."

Thoughts commingled, all right. Father and son both dwelt on them, but not a word was ever spoken about his illness and that made it worse—at least for the son. His shadow was my shadow, and apparently I was a lousy doctor. The book plundered from a drawer where I had no business presented a choice from which there was no pulling back. I could deny the physical, relegate his condition to the realm of thought where it touched us all, and attempt to save him (and us) by thinking straight. Or I could insist that his body was his own; in short, condemn him and him alone. I sacrificed him—or, more precisely, I believed that I left him to the natural world much the way Eskimos are said to abandon the old to a harsh climate with nothing but a spear and a few days' supply of seal meat. I became the sort of smart-ass child who asks, "If the mind can heal, doesn't it not also infect?"

Elsewhere Mrs. Eddy commanded deference to the laws of Caesar, a sure sign in youthful eyes that she couldn't make it on her own: "All published quotations from my works must have the author's name added to them. Quotation marks are insufficient. Borrowing from my copyrighted works, without credit, is inadmissible." Can you imagine Christ or the Gautama Buddha worrying about their billing?

Harry Greenstein phones while I'm preparing a lecture on standing, the legal doctrine used to decide who has been hurt enough to claim the law's protection. The law of standing gets complicated, with judges making metaphysical distinctions between who can sue and who can't, but laymen have surprisingly little trouble with the concept. For example, I tell Connie that my problem is a disgusting excess of both willfulness and reliability, but having married with her eyes open she has no standing. Clear?

Greenstein is not coming to the point. Between uh-huhs I gaze at the office mess. My cell is layered like an onion. A criminal-law layer, a clipping layer. Legal briefs line the shelves. Layers of student papers lie unread and ungraded amidst notes for articles that someday I will certainly write. The photographs stare back at me. Beautiful as they are, only at odd times like this do I actually look at them. The photographs have layers so dense that it is difficult to pull the membranes apart. Jeremy with Rudy and two French hitchhikers on Rhodes; with Connie and children, overlapping stages and phases. A snowy egret in flight. Famous client number one, now a Jesus freak; famous client number two, murdered a decade ago. William Butler Yeats.

Why do I have a picture of Yeats on my wall, brought back from Sligo, no less, by a friend who is a biographer of Maude Gunne? And Yeats the younger, all starched out as if he were going to a theosophy lecture at Madame Blavatsky's? To the visitor who doesn't immediately recognize the composed creamy-skinned young man in a black suit and wing collar, I suppose he looks like an ancestor. Along with his poetry, I have adopted him. Now I will have to turn the picture to the wall, the penalty of insight being the discard of illusion. A rule.

Greenstein sounds peculiar. There are long pauses while he sucks air and exhales into the mouthpiece. I met him at a group-relations conference where we studied the covert communication of people in groups by meeting in a group with covert communication. Since we raised conscious-ness by rudely interpreting hidden meanings, by speaking unmentionables, I think of Harry as a straight shooter. When the group assembled at an out-of-session women's college near the Hudson, taking old wooden school chairs arranged in a circle, someone began to go around with names. When they got to Harry, he just stared at the floor. At first they merely passed him by; ten minutes later he was consuming everyone's rage. These polite, orderly psychologists, doctors and social workers were ready to dice him like Chinese chicken. He took it silently until they tired of the game and began to ignore him. Then with an impish grin he asked his chief tormentor whether she could remember anyone's name.

But now he labors against a heavy current. "Breach of confidentiality... awkward and guilty...especially as I'm talking to a lawyer...but some things must be told, some rules made to break."

"Out with it, Harry."

A lover of his works at Cornell Medical. Word is that Manny has a tumor. Inoperable. Terminal.

I have to stroke him. "Perfectly correct...rules tempered by human val-ues.... Much better that I know.... Won't breathe a word.... The way Manny would have handled it.... Gives me a chance to say a quiet goodbye.... Gutsy on your part."

Greenstein works himself up to a few words on the ambivalence of sepa-ration but realizes his next hour is about to begin and hangs up.

Immediately I set to work in my good-patient way drafting a note to Manny. Twice a year I send him these wife-happy-kids-thriving letters, the kind I get from former students who carried something away. The envelope is sealed, the stamp is sticky on my tongue, when the sight of his address recalls the room in which I vented so much. I tear up the note.

I have learned to counteract my family's curse—that all lumps are ma-lignant, all malignancies lead to death, all death proves fatal—but I know right away, when the phone is picked up by Manny's wife, that Harry's lover was right. In five years of changing appointments the phone has been an-swered by a service or by Manny himself. So the stern woman who comes to the door of the waiting room with a mixture of frown and nod to greet her own patients actually has a voice. A woman's voice, a worried woman's voice making human noises during business hours. Then, most startling of all, facts. Facts about my shrink are rarer than emeralds in Ohio. I once saw him on a bicycle in Central Park, a treasured memory.

"The doctor has been sick, but I will see if he can speak to you."

A moment later Manny comes on. "Heavy going, but now I'm on the mend. How are things with you?"

I rush out five minutes of testimonials to our wonderful hours together; after all, he's the patient. "Lunch?" I am shocked by my daring. Lunch with my dying shrink. Is this what I've learned?

He sees through me like glass. "They've put up a new building at the hospital simply to expand the cafeteria. I'll call you when I'm a little better. Tell me, how is it the courts give those nursing-home vermin such short sentences?"

We settle on a Friday, and I keep my calendar free for the next month. No call. Each morning I find myself opening the *Times* to the obituaries, calculating the average age of death, comparing it to his, to my own. I find it difficult to end my morning jog, fall in love with a new woman every week, spend hours helping Dee with her homework. My eyes water in a movie theater, but then, I remind myself, that's nothing new. I tell Connie I have a cold.

She shrugs. "You never get colds."

I track the watermarks of these tears back to their origins in the Summer Palace, a dilapidated movie theater hard by the penny arcade and my regular Saturday afternoon destination. A movie theater is a place where children are put in jeopardy. Their screams and tears—in my case, the latter—are cries for help as the monster clumps its way up the stone staircase of the dark castle, the black-haired witch of curling lashes drops a potion in the glass of the unsuspecting visitor, the Indians spring from their perch to the arroyo. They don't always understand it's just a movie.

Finally, Greenstein calls. After going through the same preliminaries, he spits it out: "Listen, buddy, I can't sit on this. Manny is back in the hospital. Isn't seeing his friends. Refuses chemotherapy. Doesn't want the course of the disease slowed. Says the last rites of passage are barbaric."

Three days later my man has made the paper for the last time.

My cousin Philo is a therapist in Washington, having migrated there from Boston because government health insurance provides a steady supply of paying patients. He used to practice out of an old red-brick on a leafy street in Cleveland Park. When he decided to take advantage of the booming real-estate market and sell his house, he put up a huge For Sale sign on the lawn. Half his patients never mentioned it; the other half talked of nothing else for weeks. Until he moved around the corner, all their other symptoms disappeared. The last time he tried to take a vacation there were two serious suicide attempts in his Wednesday night therapy group. Manny is cremated after a private funeral. At his memorial service I learn he had a son and a regular Tuesday night poker game. I suppose I handled it very well. My SAT's must be pushing 800.

Manny should have been a formidable poker player, shrinks being so adept at wheeling emotions into place at just the right moment. Lawyers are the same way. To avoid my own kind, and because I hate to lose, my own poker game is usually populated by journalists and literati. Both tend to lack the self-discipline necessary to win, though most have a high regard for their own skill. The competition is flabby enough to permit dreamy thoughts of how everyone in this particular game is better known than I am. Fame, I conclude, helps mark our passage. In the city a brush with it allows us to remember events that otherwise would congeal. To me, the people in the room are landmarks; to them, I'm a pair of glasses that calls, raises and fills out the table. I play with characteristic alertness to every move, logging for immediate recall the variations in pitch, tone and speed of speech, alterations in posture from hunching over before a raise to leaning back before a fold, noting the number of straight bourbons drained by the hostess (three) and the Germanic mumbling of the biggest winner.

I try to distinguish cards and horses. The track is a place for an analyst. Hundreds of variables affect outcome; they must be sorted, weighed, balanced and applied in the thirty or so minutes between races. Horse racing is the sport of kings because rulers like to think of themselves as attacking problems of state in this sort of predictive mold. A leader wants to believe that his analysis of the options, not the fudged data with which he is usually presented, determines whether thumbs go up or down. Poker, on the other hand, is a game of routes; for me, at least, the logic never changes. Hands partake inevitably and unalterably of a limited number of types. I could play in my sleep with only minimal loss of skill. In poker we shuffle cards instead of papers: the sport of bureaucrats.

I am surprised at how engaged my distinguished colleagues are by the game. The only difference between me and them consists of my knowledge that the night will be memorable due solely to their presence, while they will forget it a week later. These celebrities remind me of the magical need so many of us seem to have to remember the trivia associated with the anointed few.

My college history professor, a compact white-haired man named Beely, gave unusual final exams. At the opening bell he would slip into the examination room, write a word or two on the blackboard and disappear. After the titters and awkward laughter, the chairs stopped their creaking and we contemplated "fences" or "silver" or "whale oil." In my senior year Beely gave an A+ to a mousy girl from Massillon, Ohio, who filled her bluebook with a blow-by-blow description of how she'd been held on her father's shoulders to see Wendell Willkie as he campaigned down Main Street in 1940. All Beely had written on the board was "One World."

Jackie Robinson has long passed to his well-deserved rest, but I still recall the rep tie he wore in 1953 when my father signed him to a calendar deal for a spark plug company that put his flying spikes on body-shop walls coast to coast.

The Episcopalian socialist-journalist sitting to my right gored McCarthy early with vicious pieces, allusions to his drinking, his life with Cohn and Schine, the source of the junior senator's campaign chest. I first read him in rush-hour subway cars riding home from high school. It was like finding a diamond in a box of cornflakes. The journalist persuaded his publisher that McCarthy was a climber and a fraud; the publisher resisted the demands of patriots that he be fired. The publisher dined out on a story of throwing two FBI hoods out of his office, but six months later he suddenly asked the journalist to leave when a department store executive pulled an ad. The journalist abandoned daily papers, moved to Washington and wrote curious magazine pieces studded with references to papal bulls and eighteenth-century British parliamentarians. Women hate his stuff; the sentences are too indirect, elaborate concoctions, something out of a male tent from which they are barred. In a contest between WASP guilt and Jewish guilt he holds his own. Often I see him trudging around the West Side, carrying a shopping bag filled with papers and books, looking intently into the smoke from his pipe.

I read the famous critic while cutting classes. His reviews held more than the movie, book or play. Ideas radiated out like streets from an Umbrian piazza. He had well-known alliances, never an unpublished wife or mistress. His play was aberrant. In guts poker he'd open under the gun with a low pair or pull for an inside straight after bumping the pot. He looked for case tens. He raised on prospects, then abruptly folded. I didn't like it; he wasn't following the rules. I think he did it to ward off defeat. Uncertain of his tactics, he resorted to open self-deprecation. But he may just have been playful. His nervous smile said: "You know, it's only a game." Well, each man his own front.

The riddle is my search for settled standards, right answers and most of all continuity when all the hearts I know, my own included, are a mess. Here is a plausible explanation: in this city our pace is jagged, our spirit fractious. My feelings come in spasms. We move in the reactive, impersonal manner of blips on the screen of one of those electronic games you plug into a television monitor or play in a bar. Our strip of light goes blip, blip across the field, bangs into another, then blip, blip, blip off in a new direction. Continuity allows us to penetrate the machine, to discover a human purpose in the blips. Judges, however, should be certain where they are headed. They have put away childish things; they play for keeps. Plato put them over those subversives, the poets, to rule them.

I suppose it doesn't matter, poets and judges being of the same class. Sometimes in the winter we're joined in our game by Ike Parnell, one of Fritz's clients, a free lance who shuttles between the city and a commune near Brattleboro to bring us perspective. Ike says I have the wrong vocabulary. The blips have nothing to do with a fragmented inner life, look instead to the sources of prestige and honor. The struggle that counts is over who gets to occupy limited space, who is let in and who is kept out—most of all, who *decides*. He tells me to read Max Weber. Everything is in Weber, he says, if only we'll look.

I once sat in a class with a hundred and forty others taught by the famous law teacher. He told us of preparing the will of a rich client. It had gone through a dozen drafts, each returned for a minor revision. With a senior partner he took the final, approved version, typed on paper as thick as parchment, bound with a red velvet ribbon, to the client's Park Avenue apartment. They sipped ancient sherry and discussed the weather. Whenever the senior partner tried to get the document signed, he was offered more to drink. The old millionaire insisted on keeping the will overnight and returning it by messenger. He never signed; as a consequence, the government took half his estate in taxes. The class booed. One other thing about the famous law teacher: I had slept with his daughter.

I don't like Dee to see me smoke, though I never actually hide it from her. I smoke in my office, alone mostly. Smoking in public is a weakness. At faculty meetings no one smokes anymore. It's a social revolution. These lawyers all know never to show a flaw—unless you get something by doing it. I've been shamed out of smoking at these meetings. The doctor Manny sent me to said I didn't smoke too much. "At your age we worry more about heart attacks." He puffed away, still alive at sixty-eight. I held this image as a charm, something between me and the niche.

The television producer across the table once wrote an angry letter to the *Times* about smoking. His father, he said, had killed himself on the weed, and it made him angry to see Congress let the tobacco industry get away with murder. He had solved his problem by finding the enemy outside of himself; his anger kept him happy. I admire the man. I've remembered the letter for an unaccountably long time, but when we play poker together I can't bring myself to tell him I read it. The small professor of criminology with the gentle German accent tells the hostess how much he enjoys her books. She replies that poker with him delights. But I'm unable to tell the producer of my admiration for his letter. The man certainly would be pleased. Who remembers five-year-old letters to the *Times?* But I cannot approach that righteous indignation.

At a gallery opening the girl asks how a court might be induced to declare Nixon's bombing of Cambodia illegal. Halfway through a difficult explanation she loses interest in both me and her question, and excuses herself to join a group surrounding the famous politician. I take my revenge by never voting for him.

The tic to the famous playwright is as tenuous, but the impact has been greater. I read her memoirs before they became fashionable and shared them with a woman who later offered love. I returned the favor.

We have an unspoken rule against shop talk. No one mentions serious ideas or mutual friends. Sailboat racing is an approved topic. The playwright occasionally complains that poker chips have deteriorated. In her father's day they were ivory. She absent-mindedly fingers the serrated blue and white plastic and forgets to ante. When she says "rat-fuck," the table rings with laughter.

Ultimately the game is a great equalizer, the cards remaining unaffected by who handles them. The famous play with such pleasure because the rules and rituals of the table permit them to proceed as they are, not as armies of their admirers need them to be. They play for relief, while I, having nothing to avoid, feel free to expand beyond recognition. Dee has learned that I always return from this particular night with money in my pocket. The next morning at breakfast she sidles up to her old dad and, employing her best caricature of a sitcom teenager, begs for a cut. I fork over generously, but not until I've made the point that all the players came out ahead.

City

AT AN East Side party I meet a sleep researcher, an inelegant barrel of a man who does a lot of visible deep breathing. He avoids my eyes. Teetering on the edge of Fritz's wicker couch as if he's waiting for a summons to leave, he sniffs at his whiskey like a retriever. Also poised on the edge of something, I inquire after his work. To avoid career choices—implying as they do that my life story makes sense—I interview. I am a tape recorder, buttons depressed.

"We induce psychosis," he tells me, "by blocking dreams. Technicians monitor signals from electrodes attached to the heads of sleeping subjects. When their EEG announces a dream, they are awakened." After a night of this the students he recruits for these experiments twitch and fiddle, turn irritable and anxious. Gently rotating the ice in his glass, my companion blandly reports that the males are soon incapable of erection. "Without dreams," he says, looking at me for the first time, "there is nothing."

I forget the conversation but wake up a week later in the middle of the night with a fist clenched around my prick. Untangling from the sheets, leaving Connie safe in her cocoon, I make my way to the toilet. As the flood of urine dashes the bowl I wonder: if dreams keep us from derangement and impotence, is sex only a wakeful dream? In my lust I jostle Connie awake. She is alarmed but does not complain. "In sort of wakeful swoon, perplexed she lay."

There were three options: fly to Puerto Rico, drive to the famous Quaker in Pennsylvania or taxi to Brooklyn. Before Amy settled on Flatbush, we had several "I don't care, you decide" conversations. Feeling responsible for the cause but not the effect, I couldn't decide anything except that it was cowardly for me not to be present. The doctor told her this was out of the question. Feeling as if I'd been excused from a final exam, I took her as far as the quiet residential street and waited at the corner as she climbed the steps of the brownstone. Before entering the vestibule, she pulled off her scarf and shook her hair heroically. I turned toward the subway, sure she would die. The imagined police car never came to block my path to Manhattan.

My only charge was to get an apartment. Binni was married to Tom then, and I bought them a weekend at Montauk. They were happy to go and on their best behavior, like people doing a small service for the bereaved family—though later Binni let me know that I forgot to clean vomit from the bathroom tiles. Amy was sitting in the hallway looking at her hands when I opened the door. I helped her to the bed. "Oh, Christ," she rasped, "he must have used sandpaper." When the Demerol wore off, she scratched the sheets with her nails, crawled into a little ball and pushed her head into the pillow. In a prim nightgown, showing little more than ankles and wrists, she looked as frail as a sick child. She offered no details, and I couldn't bring myself to ask. I made tea and stroked her back. We barely talked. Unbelievably, while she slept I thought about her apple breasts.

A month later she sent me a check for half the cost. She had wanted to pay for it all. "My lapse," she said. Afterwards I would get regular calls asking advice from worried friends of friends. They were grateful to talk with a man of experience. A few years later the cops raided the doctor and the state took away his license. According to the alumni magazine, Amy is teaching in Arizona.

My parents decided to move back to Manhattan just as the tide was flowing to the suburbs. On the bus little gangsters extorted dimes. Anyone without a satin jacket was fair game. I was big for my age, and it was assumed that I was a Rambler, Turk or Purple Dragon whose armor had been left at the dry cleaners. A third of my school was black, a third Hispanic, a third Jewish—a mix which effectively simulated Levantine politics. Avoiding the feared taunt "I'll deck ya after school" required organization. Here I learned for the first time that the worst-off Americans are those who are not members of a group. For the combined, the law is a feather; for the individual, it weighs a ton. Hence the policy of those in authority to keep those they wish to control far apart.

The Jewish gang, called the Loan Sharks, convened to plan strategy at the Hole in the Wall delicatessen on Broadway. Shelly proposed secret alliances with both the black and Puerto Rican factions. His policy was to send emissaries to the enemy camp suggesting a basketball tournament. With Rubin's slick one-hand jump shot and my height, he expected to gather in a large pool of side bets. But leaving the court after the Sharks' first victory, Shelly was set upon and beaten with a pipe, his nose fractured, lip cut, eyes bloodshot for weeks. We heard the rumor that the starting center on the other team was the son of the neighborhood bookie, who disliked being cut out of the action. The Sharks also walked up West End Avenue drinking

Cold Duck and smoking.

A disciplinarian, Mrs. Kelly the homeroom teacher, kept us late, dismissal contingent on writing a three-page essay on a subject of our choice. Mine was on the folly of keeping us after school to write essays, followed by the honor of being the first Jewish boy ever to be suspended. New respect from the Puerto Ricans. In shop, however, my bench-mate, Josie, the pitcher on the class hardball team, asked me to hold a soldering iron. I turned blindly. He laid the smoking iron across my palm and smirked. I ran downstairs, hailed a cab crosstown and barged into my doctor's office, where the nurse, whose uniform I had dreamed of taking off many a tossing night, cradled the hand in her lap and applied salve and bandages.

The next day Josie wanted to be my friend. What could I do? Hitting him would have upset the balance of power and brought on nuclear war, which I knew all about because every morning we spent thirty seconds under our desks during the take-cover drill that followed the pledge of allegiance. I concentrated on looking at the protective thighs under the skirt of Miss Rama, the Spanish teacher. I never met my first love, a twelve-year-old girl from Queens who, the *Post* said, refused to take cover. According to the ACLU lawyer defending her against expulsion, Brenda believed civil-defense drills fostered the illusion that New Yorkers could survive an atomic attack. In order to keep us in line, Mrs. Kelly alluded often to our pink Permanent Record Card held in the principal's office but reported to follow us to the grave. Oblivious to the entries on her Permanent Record Card, Brenda seemed a Joan of Arc.

Because he looked like an Olympic wrestler, Zeno the Greek was admitted to the Sharks, though not to the inner circle. We chipped in to buy him a jacket and deployed him as a bouncer, a deterrent to scare away the enemy. In those days, before heroin substituted flight for fight as the prime motive of gang affiliation, military considerations loomed large in our thinking. But it would be a mistake to attribute the fate of my generation to a fear of nuclear incineration. Social analysts and editorial writers who subsequently chalked up to The Bomb the rebellion of the sixties must have come of age in the outlying of those concentric circles that the newspapers used to print, circles that designated with each five-mile arc from the Empire State Building an increasing percentage of putative survivors after a direct hit. Having lived both in the inner city, where we were expected to sizzle on an incandescent grid, and on the fringes, hypothetically exposed only to serious burns and blindness, I found the influence of doomsday thinking incomparably more disturbing in the "safe" areas. Living five minutes from Needle Park, crossing Manhattan daily—an hour each way—in order to attend high school, watching the unruly balcony crowd at a Ranger hockey game (in the penultimate Garden, the one on Fiftieth Street), was to know that the someone who was out to get you did not reside in the far-off Kremlin but crouched in the next seat on the subway. The telltale marks of the nurtured-in-midtown-Manhattan breed, as distinct as the indelible numbers tattooed on the lips of thoroughbreds, is a tightness in the neck that comes from anticipating danger at all times—as specific an adaptation to environment as any Darwin found in the Galapagos. A secondary symptom is massive revulsion at any effort to make over this reality by insipid, fatuous boosterism into a whore with a heart of gold, the Greatest City on Earth.

Zeno worked after school and so rarely showed up at the Hole in the Wall. He found us tame and talkative, but there were too few Greeks to form a club. Like so many immigrants before him, he became a little Jewish, and even learned not to order pastrami on white bread with mayonnaise. Zeno boasted a five-borough fighting record. In Hell's Kitchen the gangs met at night to rumble under the West Side Highway with chains, belts and tire irons; gossip had it that he had murdered an Italian loudmouth in one of these brawls. At his last school, it was said, he had flattened a gym teacher. The Sharks were ambivalent about this life, wanting to swing garrison belts but not to bleed, recognizing that manhood must include the physical but ignorant of any adult who worked with his body more than Wax's father—a route man for the Diamond Rye Bread Company. Even Shelly's father carried a clipboard as he wandered about his building replacing washers and spraying for roaches.

At that time I believed, as I still believe, that bosses and offices were far more capable of leaving me a castrato than any side-street encounter with the marauding, knife-carrying West Side Ramblers. The Ramblers came in all sizes, like olives. There were the Juniors, the Apprentices, the Talon Ramblers, and the Alumni Association. The Ramblers were adept at provoking a fight by sending in the smallest and youngest division to accost the enemy. It was only after foolishly brushing aside the pipsqueak who tripped you on the staircase that you found yourself surrounded by the Talons. But Zeno's legendary strength and total inability to reason—traits which it was in our interest to embellish—provided a partial immunity to the worst excesses of the period. This sense of security destroyed our need to collaborate. We turned from group to individual concerns, converting the cliché: not having to make war freed us to make love. At the Hole in the Wall the jokes—and thus the feeling—increasingly focused on who put out. Across speckled Formica littered with soda cans and half-eaten jelly doughnuts I saw signs of tomorrow. Rubin would become a buyer at Macy's, Bernstein a bookie, Wax an engineer and Zeno a short-order cook. Shelly was plainly headed for Albany. It was settled that I would become Brenda's lawyer.

Joe Welch resolved all doubts, demonstrating that the mind could be as brutally efficient as the body, that a man who went to work in the morning and came home to dinner could muster as much power and toughness as anyone I met east of Broadway. Joseph Welch, the fastidious, schoolmarmish, even prissy lawyer from Boston who demolished Joe McCarthy with his whiny voice, attention to detail and cadgy knowledge about what the crowd wanted in honorable men. I cut school to watch this knight in a three-piece suit joust with the devil, and though he looked as if he couldn't lift a copy of the Congressional Record, he talked like a giant, a man who could bench-press three hundred pounds with his brain.

I like Fritz, my agent, because he has a vision of what I should be and cares enough to push it. He has me captured. There have been times when I felt I was writing more for my agent than for myself—writing so he would be pleased, earn his 10 percent and, most of all, keep me a contented beast in his stable. Fritz is innocent of such thoughts, and would not believe them. He is dour and sour on a life of busted marriages, and sometimes he overreaches, but he is the best of a friend made in adulthood. No accidents of work or geography brought us together; we chose.

"Money," he says, stirring a spinach salad reminiscent of the grass in London's Green Park. "I'm against that, you know. You have enough money. Why do you need an advance to check this out?"

This time he's gone too far. "Stay in your wheeler-dealer role and leave the values to me. My money," I remind him, "is tied up in private schools, quarterly tax payments, a housekeeper, a house in the country, a trip to Europe every spring, and the shrinks—someone in my family is always seeing a shrink."

Fritz is unhappy with me. Once he was political; he got his start pushing books from the New Left, thrusting on reluctant publishers vivid ghetto memoirs written by black convicts. His interest in such texts has cooled. Now he grabs a subsidiary right as fast as the next agent, but nevertheless I've disappointed him. I'm supposed to be one of his serious people, giving balance to his list. He thinks a public-interest lawyer should at least be subtle.

"Below the belt, Fritz. You know I'm too vain to do things solely for the money. I didn't live in south Georgia for the money."

Now I'm trading on reputation and superior credentials. While Fritz has been bringing the world *How to Feel Right Through Deep Breathing and*

Meditation (thirty weeks on the best-seller list) and salting away equity in several pieces of high-yield real estate, I've been on the firing line and on the playing fields of *The New York Times*. So Fritz shuts up. My only reservation about our friendship is that I freely offer and he engagingly accepts such arrant guilt manipulation. But why is it that strong men still lecture me? Perhaps I don't look my age. Something inherited from my mother or, more likely, a need to look different from the condemned. At thirty-nine I shape up better than at twenty-nine, and at twenty-nine better than at nineteen. Still, when someone tells me I look lean and healthy, I'm sure the end is near.

The project I finagled Fritz with began at the Mount Auburn Cemetery. My mother-in-law, Mary, picked me up at Logan Airport, then drove to Cambridge in that distracting way of hers, full of near misses. On the Charles a coxswain bent in the shape of a parenthesis exhorted his crew. Mary and I talked about the children. Near Harvard Square she took an unfamiliar turn. "I want to show you something." Right away I understood. Was it a special gift that I knew, or commonplace—something people would know and simply not mention? Her eyes danced across the monuments. We picked our way through Bellwort Path, down Laurel Avenue, looking for Isabel Stewart Gardner. I spotted a hermit thrush, a few phoebes and a blur of color that had to be a yellow-bellied sapsucker.

"That's a gorgie," she exclaimed, pointing to a marble angel. The lilacs were in bloom. Except for the hearses drawn up by the gate, it would have been a wonderful spot for a picnic. Old Boston entombed with its notables. "There it is." A knoll by a pond. We left the car and stood near the plot, a lawn mower in the distance humming like a small plane. "What better place than a Victorian cemetery, don't you agree?" I pawed the grass nervously and said nothing. "Isn't it a beautiful place? Water and shade and a slight rise." She circled the plot, as if checking the metes and bounds. "I can't wait," she said, looking at her watch. "Lost track of the time. I have to pick up some groceries. Now, Jeremy, tell me all about your cases...."

Mary and I fought from the first, squabbling over who would manage Connie's soul. We pecked at Connie, pulled and hauled, leveraged the guilt. In our power game loyalty was the coin. It took years for daughter to put mother and husband in their place, to give us our just deserts. Mary and I came to tolerate each other much like enemies who have been victims of a common disaster. Coming to terms with Connie, we had to deal with each other.

Connie too is a cemetery freak. Take her half across the world, and while others sip their tea or muse in the Prado, she drifts away to wander down the quiet lanes of an old graveyard. She loved Corsica, an island populated more by the dead than the living, but there is nothing on earth, not even Père Lachaise, to compare with Mount Auburn. I hold my distance from this affection for mossy tombstones and shaded burial places; to keep my anxiety about death below the Plimsoll line, I try to interpret these two women. I see both of them as having been cut loose from a place where expectation and what was expected neatly fit and set down on the road of self definition. Having to decide what you should be is generally a pain in the ass. Too many choices are as much of a curse as too few. Uneasy with the modern woman but unwilling to pass up the brass ring of freedom, occasionally they each need to touch their own serenity; hence this graveyard aesthetic, these visits to certainty.

In most respects Mary was immune to fashion. An eccentric who refused to accept the separation of mother and daughter, she would have chosen, if it were up to her, that we all live in the same house. Her approach to death, as when she calmly displayed her grave plot like a realtor showing a particularly hot property, removed her to another age. Her attraction stuck to these differences: imagery, insistences, opinions carried from beyond the perimeter of my experience. She was more generous to strangers than to acquaintances, never referred to female anatomy and dressed for dinner.

She was a woman whose barbed consistency was inconsistency. She loved you, she hated you; she needed you, she was indifferent. She'd been denied something fundamental that overshadowed the lightning of her mind. As a young woman her passion had passed to controlling the values her children assigned to their works; thus they were occupied territory. Even now Connie can reexperience the cause, explain the result. She can avoid, deny, interpret, even purge, but since the mother-judge in her head is her character and her fate, she cannot escape. The point is, she doesn't want to. The two are one: if she eliminates her mother, nothing will be left.

Still, Connie is more difficult to pin down than her mother. Some weeks it seems she is playing the lead in a musical comedy based on the works of Hegel called something like *Once upon a Dialectic*. She wakes up at dawn Monday morning full of concern for the world around her. She pays her bills, repots plants, reads the papers and skips off to school with Denny, our little boy. For the rest of the day and part of Tuesday she runs errands, talks to editors and moves about the city, a green satchel and leather shoulder bag bouncing in her wake. By Wednesday the thesis of satisfaction with her lot as pampered upper-middle-class New York woman has been replaced by the antithesis of restless depression. In the middle of the week I shop, cook and hold down the posts of social secretary and school shlepper while

Connie broods over her typewriter and complains that we never talk about anything but schedules. On Friday we flee to the farm as if the city is under a threat of invasion by nightfall. In the country she finds peace, but the synthesis is remote, somehow irrelevant, unconnected. By lunch on Sunday she wants to get back.

"Radical lesbians," Fritz is saying, "are downers. I don't know how to sell this kind of book. In any event, what makes you think this one will talk to you? You're a man, for Chrissake."

Fritz professes to hate these traditional publishing lunches, but has never been seen anywhere between noon and two except in a midtown French restaurant. His special quality is not to have become shopworn or case-hardened. Books for him are still magic, babies that take nine months to produce from the day the manuscript arrives until pub date, children with a life of their own. Books are not clippings, reviews, cards saying "With the compliments of the author," people writing books to have author's parties. Books are holy objects. If he is indiscriminate in gathering his list, well, that just continues the sexual side of the connection; it is nature's way of making sure by excess.

As a matter of faith, Fritz takes a writer's energy where he finds it. He points out the pitfalls and makes us explain, but ultimately he goes along. For my Lavender Menace project, he'll spend some of his credit around town in order to find it a home—even though he knows I'm taking advantage of him. We both doubt whether anything will come of it. I promise myself to tell him to stick this profile of a Movement woman on the bottom of the pile; then conveniently I forget. Bad faith. The question I don't want to answer, I must remember, is why I need Fritz to certify, with an advance, an option or even a promise of interest from a serious editor, the *bona fides* of a few weeks on the road to check out this idea.

The clinical categories explaining this quest may be accurate, but without a few months on Manny's now retired couch I can't pay them much mind. *How* we learn is *what* we learn. As Mary's executor I had more to distract me than the rest of the family. Her papers and effects kept me from the general emptiness when we sat around the old house, unsure of what to do without her. The legal work forced me to keep up our fifteen-year conversation. I found one of my remaindered books next to her bed—corners of the pages turned down, grammar corrected, diction questioned, syntactical errors scored with a red pencil. I also discovered her file on the Lavender Menace, one of her former students, then poised on the cusp between front-page headlines and prison.

Perhaps I took over the project because I was secretly in love with my mother-in-law; if so, it was affection for an abstraction. Connie, who is round and brown and deft, does not resemble her angular mother, whose face jutted out to meet you like the prow of a ship. If I loved anything about that crusty, hypercritical lady who in death is now ironically my client, it was her standards. Whether in architecture, literature, music or people, she had a talent for focusing on the point of classic purity—Scarlatti, for example—and dismissing the rest. Her friends, if that was what they were, held her opinions in awe, afraid where the knife would point next; consequently, she regarded most of them as sycophants. She viewed Connie's premeditated selection of me for a mate less as rebellion than as treason. Treason, remember, implies an obligation of loyalty. By the measure of Mary's contempt, Connie might have chosen the youngest son of a Tunisian camel driver. My wife has extracted the blade, but the wound remains. She fears she will always be offering up her works, and ultimately herself, for rejection. The treason didn't change *that*. Nor did death; the circle merely narrowed down to the drama in Connie's head.

This need of marketplace approval—conning Fritz into underwriting the public value of a private journey—is the wish to get paid off for everything I do. I must start with the idea that spending our powers depletes them. The thing to do with risks is reduce them. Ergo, there is no better deal than something for nothing. Is this sly and primitive or merely common sense? All I can say is, whatever lurks in the shadows of this project, I don't want to know too much about it. And by rushing in to examine the social significance of the Lavender Menace, whatever it is, I will have no need to find out.

I expect that Fritz will kill the deal when he learns the LM once studied with Mary, but he lets it go (if you want them tough, don't choose a friend for an agent) and my fantasy of approaching Mary's gentle contemplation-of-death rebellion has too much flesh for me to drop it. If only I could have run this caper by Manny first—except I know too well what would have been the result. "So now," he would say, "you're in the resurrection business?" Leaning forward in his dark leather shrink chair to a place where I could see him out of the corner of an eye, he would twinkle. Yes, twinkle, like a summer sky seen flat on your back in the north woods. He was a short man who wore bowties, and when he knew that I knew he'd caught me in a deception he became a Walt Disney elf. Someone has said you can't buy a happy man, but how can you tell when you've found one? For me, the litmus-paper test is Manny's twinkle.

But he would take it away, and so to hell with him. The problem with psychoanalysis, even in the hands of an artist like Manny, is that all too often it forgets that the crazy side of our nature protects us from nothingness, a fate far worse than neurosis. "When you complete treatment," Manny might say of this project, using irony like a surgical instrument, "no doubt you'll want to become a therapist. Perhaps it would be better to let her go." He'd co-opt my pursuit of Mary's ghost as smartly as any politician on a breezy ghetto tour.

Death imposes forms that are beyond even Manny's boardinghouse reach. When Binni, who is a Gestalt therapist and alert to such things, went to visit her ninety-eight-year-old grandmother for the last time, the old woman told her that the Angel of Death had come to her the night before but decided not to stay. "There is someone you have to see first," the Angel insisted.

A foundation flew me first-class to a Texas conference center to talk about poverty law. They were cutting up a bequest and needed to make a record of consulting the experts before handing out the shares. Their strategy was simple and effective: afraid that the losers might gripe to Congress or the press, they brought in a planeload of politicians and academics, held a meeting, taped and transcribed the discussion and issued a report backing what they'd planned to do from the start. With the approval of so many esteemed professionals and experts, no one could find fault.

I talked intensely about ways to provide indigents with competent lawyers but failed to provoke a sit-in at the local bar association. However, it was in everyone's interest to deny that it didn't matter what was said, so papers were received enthusiastically. The female participants met and produced a list of seven demands but were thwarted when they couldn't find anyone to demand them from. To further establish that we had earned our fees, brawls broke out in the bar and factions caucused around the pool. A babe in these woods, I had neglected to ask the woman who called with the invitation about the honorarium and so was paid the same as their token Chicano.

This woman—reputed to be the benefactor's mistress—had been appointed executive secretary of the foundation. With a lifetime job, she controlled disbursements in the name of the public interest. The dead drill-bit king had been married four times. He put his billions in a charitable trust as the only discreet and legally foolproof way to settle the bundle on the most important person in his life and keep it out of the hands of pleasure-loving wives, children and grandchildren, all of whom he disliked and distrusted for their spendthrift ways. Holding court over bourbon, red-rinsed hair running down over wire glasses, the mistress enjoyed our circus—though "mistress," connoting the sexual, conveys the wrong impression. The billionaire conferred his money on this woman because she shared his office, while the wives only shared his bed. No matter how difficult, certain impulses will work their way out—or at least the rich will find a way to work them out.

Fritz arranges a deal to pay my expenses with an editor who has just switched publishing houses and needs to acquire property quickly. But first he talks No More Mr. Nice Guy.

"I'll mother you through, but then you owe me one. If there's no book in this, I want you to try a thriller."

"I never read the stuff."

"You don't have to read it to write it. Listen, people are afraid to learn the truth, they have to be teased into it and to think they're just enjoying themselves. You are going to create desperate men and disillusioned women, caught in snares beyond their control. We'll have plutonium thievery, kidnapping, transnational corruption, hired killers, anal intercourse. When they aren't looking, you'll slip in mistrust of authority; without a polemical word, you can persuade the reader that we can't let them get away with it.

"Fritz, you are totally miscast as an agent. I had no idea you were still involved. Why do you care?"

"This stuff doesn't work without a sense of place. You'll have to bounce around the world visiting far-flung plot locations, and I'll get a chance to comfort Connie."

Because there is truth in every jest, especially this one, I smile. "I knew it was something important."

"Damn straight. You want to change people? Well, this is how. They buy these books, read them, actually enjoy the experience and tell their friends. Unless you want to write a soap, there's no other way."

Musing about the language of the publishing industry—houses, property, options—and the day when book futures will trade in the Chicago pits along with soybeans and hog bellies, the similarity between book talk and widget talk, I set off to find the Lavender Menace. She is in jail awaiting trial on charges of conspiracy to kidnap Bilt Reynaldo, the famous macho actor. Sneaking up on my obsession, I start by reading the legal file. I take the papers from her lawyer's office to the conference room and try to find some space amidst the clutter. The table is carpeted with dark brown folders, lawbooks laid out around chairs like bridge hands. Behind the cover of *The Criminal Law Reporter*, a young woman is reading a popular assertiveness-training how-to-do-it. After some pleasantries she asks what's up. I tell her I'm trying to decide whether to write about the case.

"Are you a journalist?"

"A lawyer."

Judging from the speed with which the book snaps shut, she's been caught in the act. "I'm a law student, here for the summer. Because they're all so busy with the trial, I haven't been given anything to do. I'm older. I've been away from school for seven years."

She blurts this out as if it fixes her place in the world. My student years were glazed over; eyes fixed on what would happen after they ended, I failed to pay attention. When I meet people who go to reunions or who still see their classmates, I wonder what I missed. My undergraduate sentence was spent in Ohio slavishly reading everything people told me to read, drinking 3.2 beer and scheming to avoid parietal rules. A strange place, given what we usually think of as the university life in these United States. Dubbed Tibet U. by the acolytes, run in the name of ideas and a fast-disappearing clean-cut religiosity, it was so remote from New York that I felt I'd entered a monastic order. But they took their brand of ecumenical intellectualism seriously; no hint of commerce intruded. The ultimate sins were pop music and frivolity (defined to include copulation). A thousand of us were marooned thirty miles from the nearest city, one whose cultural center was the Greyhound bus terminal. Students were forbidden to marry without decanal permission; cars were banned; liquor was illegal, grass unheard of. As winter was evicted by summer, the weather sealed us in.

More women than men applied. As a result, the females were brighter and more personable, and the marginal male plodders couldn't cope with them. Hungry junior and senior women appraised the incoming class like buyers at a Kentucky yearling sale. We were penned in, thrown back on our unformed selves, suicidal and depressive. Cliques formed, hardened and talked themselves out through the frigid winter. Incest prevailed. After four years there was no one left to screw or fall in love with; the odd man or woman out silently went crazy. Marriages not officially consummated until graduation were forced by a mutual need for survival. The kids I teach now see themselves as workers; they resist experiment and, find little compensation in mistakes. Their attitude says punch my ticket and get on with it. But at least they don't get married because they're talked out and there's nothing else to do.

I succumb. "Why did you go to law school?"

She warms to it. "Because I found that I could only get shit jobs with a B.A. and my shit days are over. I have an illegitimate child. Have to support myself."

Well, now she's declared herself. She wants to mix and mingle, but I have to accept her credentials at the start—the legitimacy of illegitimacy—or else she'll find it too scary.

"What do you think about the LM?"

She tosses her head back and her mouth begins to smile, but she comes on taut. "It's okay to be political if the politics grow out of warmth toward other people, but hers are all rebellion. Down with daddy, down with everything."

I take in the comfortable hills and valleys under her camouflage of mannish slacks and jacket, the exciting amber hair falling over her ears, a face that flushes slightly as she races on. I plan to be good for once, and not piggishly inject lustful concerns in this, ahem, professional situation, but from the start I am corrupted: the reason I'm here is to toy with Mary's curious sexual identification with the Lavender Menace.

On she goes. "One thing that makes me mad is the PR. All she did was botch the kidnapping of some box-office type, and now she's telling the world it was done to advance the women's revolution. What does a lesbian kidnapping a movie actor have to do with feminism? With the FBI combing the city and frightening a lot of women who don't want their parents or employers to know how they're living, she's even brought the cops down on her own kind. I don't care how symbolic Reynaldo is."

I push the file away, but the table is so covered with debris that it keeps slipping back toward me.

"All right, she's very sharp, I'll give you that. Disciplined. She must have been, to stay so long underground. But there's a lazy, spoiled child inside. Have you read the poetry they're showing? No distance. Sentimental crap. Arc you going to do a book on her?"

"Sometimes I judge what I'm going to write by the look of the pages in the typewriter. Hers look like e. e. cummings poems, half-thoughts marching in uneven columns. I'm finding out that militant lesbians disturb me; they upset my expectations even though, or perhaps because, I look down on them. And they're the hardest case—today's niggers, kikes and spies— so I should be out there hustling for them. At least I should have a little empathy."

"What quaint liberalism. Do you always talk so freely?"

On a yellow legal pad I've copied what looks to be a fragment of a novel from Mary's file on the LM.

A woman with magic thoughts about male power. Males decide the important issues in her life...whether she stays or goes, is secure or insecure, is loved or not. Combined with these feelings, the apprehension that she will be betrayed by males (or is it merely people in power over her?). This mistrust is a hedge, a copout permitting her not to trust her friends, her therapist, not to share feel-

ings; to withhold.

Her fantasy is that things will happen merely by her going through the forms. Without work, effort, or pain. For example, merely talking to a therapist will confer nurture, rewards, growth on her. To her. She will again be acted upon rather than act.

She is angry at herself. She expects, wishes and sometimes provokes anger from others, but it is very difficult for her to express or acknowledge feelings of anger and disapproval toward persons in male roles, in authority. Men. She dislikes it when men fail—as it suggests that they won't be able to take care of her. When a man she is seeing is close to other women, she gets upset, feels threatened, expects to be abandoned. Or her man's other life, his work, is a threat. She wants him to report, specifically, what he is up to. A friend's husband has had an affair, and the woman calls him daily to find out whether he is about to leave her. She is depressed by the husband's conduct as well as the wife's. Will she too be left, degraded?

Perhaps it is better for the friend to leave her husband before he leaves her. The greatest fear is of betrayal and loss. I hear her say women must act first.

But the act was violent, a refusal to take on another's pain as her own. Mary was working in the opposite direction, exploring the psychology of a woman—of women—by coming to terms with the LM, the Lavender Menace inside.

"Do you always come right out of the gate telling about your illegitimate child?"

"Well, aren't *we* being defensive."

We're sitting amidst the litter, deciding that intimacy without loyalty has its problems.

Later we drive through empty streets, chatting about our next move. "Kinda hard for me to decide," she says. "I've been off men for months. No, not totally. I have a friend who has a nonmonogamous marriage, but my last unrequited love ended in December."

It's only twelve-thirty, but Chinatown is deserted. Night court is in recess. A few whores are standing by an empty parking lot. I laugh to myself, remembering that it's the lot used by court personnel.

"I got this car from my parents. I've made peace of a sort. I'm all they have and they're all I have. Do you have any problem coming home with me?"

"I don't have a crisp answer."

"I understand. That's okay, perfectly all right. I keep thinking of your body. It will be a strange body, and I'm bleeding like a pig. This is the middle of the month and I have an IUD. What's your arrangement with your wife?"

"Arrangement?"

"Well, have you decided that you both do these things, or are you the only one who does them?"

I've been here before. All at once I'm suppressing a yawn, deciding I like her, and wondering if she'll make me feel guilty. "We have no arrangement."

"That's the stupidest thing I've ever heard." She makes a sharp left, throwing me against the door, and stops at a red light. "What good is that? Why bother? Shit. Next you'll be telling me you're doing it for her benefit."

Some people have this marvelous ability to be very angry and feel very deeply, but still not alienate. Cars are honking, but she takes her time moving out.

"I like living with her, I can't imagine not."

"You're corrupt."

"I suppose. The question is whether it puts you off." She swings onto the bridge, aiming for Brooklyn Heights, looking for a restaurant where she can buy an exotic drink. "Your wife must need you more than you need her. If there was equality of power, this wouldn't go on. You'd have to work it out."

She parks on a dark street filled with brownstones. The door is open, and we thread our way through cartons of unpacked books to the dining room. One of her house-mates is trying to hang a bike in the closet. I stand behind her and push the front wheel up on a hook near the ceiling. I tell her she'll have to grow taller to get it down. She shrugs like an old friend and offers me dope.

The LM reminds me more of a bouncy nursery school teacher than a violent feminist, strident lesbian, amazon menace. Thick hips show through the sagging, oversized prison pants; she is squirrel-faced. I find it difficult to think of her as a kidnapper. She must have carried the .357 Magnum with two hands. Yet she pressed the trigger. The actor had not come home that night; she and her girlfriend wounded his houseman before disappearing onto the FBI's most-wanted list for a year. The girlfriend is still at large. Ever anxious to distinguish between criminals and the rest of us, the cops gave out that an ex-con, former lover, taught her about guns. A reporter on the case has popularized the theory that bitterness toward the parolee turned into a general anger against all males.

But the few shards left in Mary's files suggest a blend of personal and political. Fallen behind the back of a drawer was a photograph of one of the students shot at Kent State. A note was appended in Mary's handwriting: "Her sexual experiences astonish me. Today she told of being 'busted' after she kissed her lover in a gay bar. At first the police informed her that she was under arrest for sodomy, though actually they seem to have charged her with disorderly conduct. At the station house, a good-looking young cop with a mustache stuck a fist in his pocket. 'What you need,' he said, 'is a big prick.' Another told her he had a piece that would make everything right. Doesn't such crudeness turn lesbians against the patriarchy?"

A dozen women wait for court to open. Wearing jeans, with cropped hair cut butch and femme, they greet each other with exaggerated hugs and kisses, cluster in the hallway and keep their distance from the reporters. Their fragility dissolves when I approach. Hard stares and monosyllables meet my questions. This is the group that has felt the brunt of the investigation; some have been visited at work. The LM appears from the lockup. They break their huddle as she parades past, hands cuffed behind her, in a line of six on the way to court. Her smile is coy; she could be graduating. Out in the audience parents and friends are watching her take the diploma. Her look says, Isn't this funny—me up here, who would have thought?

After she passes, a young girl with DYKE neatly stenciled in white on her purple T-shirt rushes toward the courtroom door. The women crowd in behind, taking seats near the defense table. When the LM enters, they stand and raise their fists. Her eyes travel to each face; she nods and takes in the next.

The Lavender Menace pleads guilty in return for a government promise not to use the grand jury to ask about her accomplice. Later she is high, chatty about prison but wary about the past. Any nervousness she might feel is well hidden. I tell her she looks confident.

"Well, I'm surrounded by loving people. We've had some strikes up there over privileges. Got them to put up a clock. We didn't have a way to tell the time. I asked three different matrons the time and got three different answers. We see movies and TV, but they lock us up between six and seven when the news is on. I don't think it's political, just thoughtlessness. Some of the guards are decent, a few hostile. Mainly it's bureaucratic."

I ask about the actor.

"The pricks will put up with us unless we really grab them and yank. We have the political understanding. Women often do. What we don't have is the means to implement it. So we made a start Sure it was a symbolic act. I had no illusion of success—at least in the short term. But I led them a merry chase, you have to admit."

I have come to see whether the New Woman cares, whether she will bring some love to her dependents, but the signals are mute and contradictory, the star still too far away for my feeble instrument to decipher its greeting. Still, she has a sense of humor, not a trait you would glean from the poetry or the rhetoric.

Perhaps for Mary's sake she doesn't seem to hold my gender against me. "It's all very simple, my friend. Everything is political if we want to see it that way. Personal acts are political acts. Personal omissions are political acts, too. Mary was beginning to understand that before she died. I took a leap she'd refused to take years earlier. We were both male-defined women, and I decided to break out. I think she was fascinated by that. She must have identified with me, but she was no closet gay. She had as much sense of how women make love as a five-year-old. Her interest was more emotional than physical. So if you're here to defend her honor, forget it."

"What about those stories in the papers about castration?"

"Some insecure newspaperman's fantasy—though I won't deny we thought of it. We were after a ransom. Finance the revolution from the pigs' pockets. It's been done in Europe for years but never caught on here. Anyway, his thing would have been left intact."

A guard comes to tell me the hour is up. I promise to return, but her look says don't bother. I probably won't because I've got my story: comfortable confirmation of my speculation that Mary was learning, even at the end, how not to obey her inner orders. But Mary's motives still confuse me. Maybe they're supposed to. If I remain confused, I hold out the possibility of the unexpected, uncontrolled, unknown. There are times when uncertainty is immensely preferable to our sievelike rational arrangements. But do I have the courage of this conviction? Would I vote for a politician who answered "Search me" when asked how he would bring peace to the Middle East, reduce unemployment *and* inflation, transform the South Bronx? What will I say to Slade?

My notebook contains a few more spare facts. In the two years before she died, Mary spent hours with this girl and a tape recorder. In my study is a shoebox where now I keep the cassettes wedged among my books. The box once sat on a brass candlestand that Connie and I bought for next to nothing when an Episcopal church sold out and followed its flock to Westchester. It took months of rubbing with steel wool and rags covered with Noxon before we found the brass beneath the wax and grime. Connie was pregnant and tired easily. She wanted to close the bedroom door and sleep, but I made her stay with me while I turned grit into gold.

With a tiny exception the tapes had been erased. I auditioned every hour of crinkly static, hoping that suddenly a door would open on human voices. Once it did. For a split second I heard Mary say the word "possible"; then the door shut as abruptly as it had opened. There is no way of telling if the erasure hid a prefix.

Other clues came from my excavations in Mary's files, but the most revealing, Connie's discovery of a journal under a quilt on her mother's bed, predates death. Opening it at random, she read a description of Mary's time in New York many years earlier, copy-editing for a book publisher before she married. Connie says the journal was filled with second thoughts, attempts to imagine the course of paths her mother never took. The perfectionist Cambridge lady I knew, who explained this year by saying that she dreamed of being Maxwell Perkins, seems once to have been an active Trotskyite. Connie felt she was on the brink of learning even more astonishing secrets when Mary entered the room, gave the culprit a gentle kiss on the forehead and retrieved her notes. "Nothing is quite so fascinating," Mary said, "as the commonplaces of a parent's life—before the child is born, that is." They never spoke of it again.

After moving to Boston, Mary lectured on American intellectual history at Radcliffe. Time off for children. Published a little here and there, mostly on the history of the prison. She charted the twisted idealism in the early nineteenth century that gave rise to the Elmira movement. Give the penitent felon time to reflect on his evil ways, keep him from the sordid influence of society, and eventually he'll be ready to join the human family. She told the story, passed no judgment—oddly for her—and left the interpretations to others.

Several years before she died, Mary and her daughter signed a neutrality pact, a cordon sanitaire. Connie put it to her bluntly: leave off or forget me. Her mother's response was to capitulate. She stopped needling Connie's ladies'-page journalism. They observed the forms: daughter showed up when daughter was supposed to; mother played grandma.

About this time I began to compete with Connie over parenting. If my work suffered, I am unaware of it, but it is undeniable that I used the knife less often and kept my elbows tucked in even after an adversary had tried to trip me up. The main casualty was the lust for litigation, the only social form available to me where meanness was legitimate. Not having to be nice, I was free to spend as much time as I wanted—long after the air conditioning was shut off, Lithuanian cleaning ladies pushing their wagons and mops through the midtown halls—flailing at the bastards. I was fortunate. I had chosen well. It was a superior sublimation because they really were bastards.

On a winter night in the early years of practice Rudy and I had taken our wives to the movies at one of those East Side houses where, abused by ushers, you stand out in the cold for forty minutes waiting to be let in. When the line finally began to move toward the door, a young couple tried to slip in unnoticed. "It's all right with me if you crash," I told the male, but not before us." He, of course, took the challenge and kept moving toward the doors. Choosing my victim carefully, I tossed him out into Third Avenue. Connie was embarrassed. Rudy shook his fist in the girl's face and told her he was going to cut off her tits. I was contrite, exhilarated and angry at having to justify myself to Connie. I don't remember the movie. I wish Rudy had been kinder to the girl. It was annoying to realize that I wouldn't have touched the kid if he'd been black.

Litigation was the pillow I beat. Then came Manny; then parenting. The pillow hasn't been quite so necessary. A late second child is a chance to reconnoiter your own childhood at leisure. I keep a book on my small son. The Brown Book, we call it, an old accountant's ledger with pages stiff as cardboard, crumbling at the edges. When Denny blandly asserts, "I'm not crying, I'm whining," or "Dad, that toast is pitch-white," I record his words, faithful as Boswell. His gift to me is irresponsibility, a time of life that had been forgotten.

Once I watched Denny and his class crowd against the far wall of a playground, making sure they touched, swarming like bees. Between them and the near side were two ten-year-olds, wiggling in place, tempting the younger ones. At a signal the mob raced apprehensively across the divide, mocking terror. The ten-year-olds reached out to capture the kindergarten as it rushed by, but the rules prohibited them from moving and they rarely succeeded. Denny is not alone in loving this game, in showing a confident smile of victory as he eludes the monsters and returns to safety.

My friends think the anger is gone. They seem fond of talking about how I've changed. I don't dispute them; the truth is, however, I'm afraid of what will take its place. My fantasy is of fury crouching behind a door, gathering strength for some heroic final assault.

Here is another note from Mary's grave:

If Jews arrive through moral works, homosexuals through aesthetics, then what synthesis is born in a lesbian Jewess from the suburbs who writes bad poetry and talks feminist Franz Fanon? Will nothing come of it unless women are violent? I try to explain her from her background but don't get very far. Father, a Long Island manufacturer, a self-made man who refused to sell his business to a conglomerate. Mother spends her days worrying over a house, buying wall-to-wall carpeting and French provincial lamps made in North Carolina, obsessed with emptying ashtrays. An older brother, a lawyer somewhere. She detests her brother but is short on details. Father and brother, she says, are excited by equipment: their weekly bang is to return from Sears with a power saw, a lathe and the latest-model trash masher.

I spend more time at work in order to evade Slade's message until a blizzard immobilizes me. Then my life becomes unbearably complicated. Snow in New York can reassure—especially in the Park, where kids soak the hillside to make a hundred-yard ice run. Down they slide, on toboggans, sleds, flattened cartons, even old toilet seats, to veer off breathless seconds before the chain-link playground fence. Even when they crash, the laughter is louder than the tears. Except for the rush to the market for bread and milk, the machine stops.

"They're not holding New York today," a lady I've never noticed before says in the elevator. But by the third day we're restless; the vacation should be over. Plows have buried the cars, roads are slick. At street corners, beyond the property line, the way is impassable. The mayor's office, deluged by calls from tenants with frozen pipes, declines to issue the daily press release claiming that New Yorkers can take anything. The networks show tapes that make the outer boroughs look like isolated Himalayan villages. The usual chorus of complaints from Queens; old people freeze to death in the Bronx; kids have killed a motorist on West Sixty-fifth Street by dropping a slab of ice from an overpass (JUST FOOLIN' ROUND is the *News* headline). Loathing sets in; the self mingles with the crud stamped into the sooty banks of ice. Near my building a plow has deposited a mountain of frozen gray-speckled slush half as tall as the awning. Near a squashed yogurt container a high-jumping setter has left its turds, proof of a climb to the summit. We can flee inward or accept the world as a mirror—either/or, the usual accommodations not being possible. On the third day job feelers from California and Washington join the judgeship on the scales of indecision.

Usually I diddle with these things just long enough to capture a good daydream: a desk free of the paper I've never learned to throw out; new paths to wear down. A man who walks a field knows from the broken grass whether he takes the same way; here our ruts are hidden by concrete. In Palo Alto my friends bike to work; in D.C. they all own agencies; in Boston they claim to hold intelligent conversations. I see myself in command, suggestions taken as orders, a simple system where pieces come together. In college we were required to attend Meeting once a week. The entire student body crammed into the chapel. I have no recollection of any word spoken at these gatherings, except gripes that we were under compulsion. But I do remember that we were all there.

My first mistake is to seek counsel from my boss. The Soft Killer asks whether I have sufficiently internalized the aggressor to sit in judgment; he wonders whether I can put up with the tedium of leadership. He laughs and rubs palms together with glee: after I resist temptation, I will be even more appreciative of his oyster. He will bleat these proposals—and Slade's message—about in the manner of a father proud of his daughter's suitors. Having clawed his way from Washington Heights to Park Avenue, he has no doubts. His children are valuable and stay near home, not as a result of anything he does but because they are his children. He will make my shifting from leg to leg a public event.

I have been working on my feelings toward the Soft Killer. He certainly gets things done. Maybe that's the problem. He gets them done by keeping us all in our place, keeping us fragmented; only he knows what the whole looks like. I worry that I must prefer his style of leadership because I don't object very loudly. None of us does. He raises the money, holds the hands, trims the budget, mediates the disputes, strokes the egos, keeps me feeling that I could have done worse—a lot worse. But I'm not happy being managed. We talk to each other only through him; when he leaves a meeting, the dialogue turns fuzzy. I'd feel better with someone who had a point of view, even one I disagreed with. The Soft Killer is not one point of view, but many. He finds the middle of every loaf and slices. I never leave his office without wondering what I haven't been told. When I get from him everything I want, I'm sure I should have asked for more. Perhaps this is where the hostility comes from: he has raised to an art the capacity for dealing that I recognize in myself.

He is also showing me that from on high it is a question of keep them apart or they'll hurt you. We set up our bosses not only to tear them down but to begrudge them. The Soft Killer possesses that rarest of qualities, competence; he sees to my needs, and yet part of me is dissatisfied. Which is why his target is never still. For him, every day is spent with someone's paranoia. The flying administrator, doomed to sail forever through seas of paper with no fixed star as a guide. Blown along by subtle distinctions, constantly checking the wind, he has no destination I can make my own.

General Spatz, Sam's chief at the agency, is so busy jetting to Geneva, quietly briefing the senators who count and sneaking into the White House, that most of his staff have never seen him. When Spatz has to take a position on the efficiency rating of plutonium recycling in light-water reactors, the number of missile-carrying submarines under construction in the Baltic or the treatment of political prisoners in South Africa, Sam's section drafts the statement without consulting him.

Then comes the fun. Nothing goes upstairs unless all the players have signed off. Sam sends the memo around. After each bureau decides what it can squeeze for itself from this one, he starts getting calls insisting on changes in the circulated draft. If the memo has implications for something important—like the number of people who can be placed on the delegation to an international negotiation in London—a bureau may append its own version to Sam's original. With every dip of the tallow, the wax thickens. When the mound of paper can no longer he carried, the players meet to hassle. As the man who can veto Sam's move today needs his signature to-morrow, they must deal. But Sam has to make concessions to preserve what he really wants. In fact, he has stuffed his policy proposal with giveaways; civil servants shake the tree and are hit with his papier-mâché apples.

When the draft has been revised for the tenth time, when all the malcon-tents have decided to acquiesce because next time they'll need Sam, Spatz gets a terse memo delineating the position that the entire agency agrees he should take. His views have not been sought; no one would gain from that, least of all Spatz, who doesn't know what he thinks about half these matters apart from what the agency tells him. Spatz, however, is more than a front man. He drives the car but has no idea what's under the hood. His schedule permits two minutes to scan the three-page memo that has been purged of all dispute before he gets his turn to be powerful. He approves or bucks it back.

Sam is trying to do something about South Africa. He wants American capital pulled from a country that spends twenty times more to educate a white child than a black, and where a black man needs a permit to live with his wife. He knows that businessmen get nervous when the State Depart-ment withdraws economic attachés, cuts back on investment credits and deliberates over export licenses. But floating a get-tough-with-the-Boers policy that makes it all the way to Spatz's desk has nothing to do with the morality of apartheid. Sam pockets the okay of a holdover bureaucrat from the last administration by signaling that his office won't press for three new slots at budget time; the general counsel comes aboard when Sam strokes his rabbi, an Indiana congressman whose biggest worry is an airbase that the Department of Defense has been threatening to close ever since the Korean war. He pacifies the chief of the technical office, a Mozart freak, by reminding him that the Afrikaaners have excluded blacks from *Don Giovan-ni* at their new opera house. After Sam gets his memo cleared, the whole business begins again on an interagency level where he must satisfy the claims of diplomats, soldiers and spooks. No wonder Washington's greatest indoor sport is the meeting. Sam thrives at this hauling and tugging. He is a still-believer; in the sixties he won battles and has never gotten over it. But he wants a partner, someone who will keep score and help him hatch bigger conspiracies against the bureaucracy.

In the end the White House takes a harder line against the denial of civil liberties in Soweto. The President includes two paragraphs in a speech to a chamber of commerce, and the press picks it up. The commercial attaché returns home for a month of consultation. The temperature has gone up a degree. It wouldn't have happened without Sam; it might have happened sooner, or even better, if we'd been working together. It cannot be done without the hauling and tugging; there is no other way. I am good at it. Sam's ends are my ends. I would do what he does. The difference is conviction. I do these things because I did them yesterday; Sam is a still-believer.

Golden Fields is one of thirty law schools looking for new deans. The old ones depart gladly, worn out after a few years of trying to cajole a group of law teachers into agreeing on anything. With tenure to teach until they turn seventy, and students so confused that they've learned mostly the lesson of obedience, law faculties have as much incentive to change as city employees would have to put their pension rights on the ballot. Only five years old, Golden Fields, they say, is different: out to make its reputation producing public lawyers of conscience. The post-Watergate law school.

But I am skeptical—jaded by New York, where problems are too large for solution and can only be managed. Take Clare's last job. She did crisis-intervention work at the Family Court. She put together a team of go-getters. Her social workers knew every decent placement in the city, and her shrinks wanted to change the system so badly that they worked for half pay. When a wayward kid was sent back to his family, a network of paraprofessionals stayed on top of the case; her team was interested in performance, not precedence. It didn't last. The probation people were furious because she might put them out of a job. Financed by soft federal money that didn't fit in the organizational chart, Clare's people were loathed by the clerks. So taken were her team members by their mission that they examined every case as if it were an original rather than a type. As a result, the clerks set records losing files. The chief judge worried about the "case-clearance ratio," as well as civil war in his domain. The mayor's office tried to place clubhouse relatives in no-show jobs. When the grant ran out, the operation folded. "Better that than keeping the shell," says Clare, "after the nut has been eaten."

Another war story: in the early sixties a group of reformers focused attention on the money bail system. If you make bail, they release you as a good risk, the sort who is likely to return. If not, you're detained and treated like a criminal. A rich man became interested when he learned to

his amazement that there were men awaiting trial in the Tombs solely because of poverty. Imagine! Ransom was inconsistent with his dim understanding of the law. Perhaps he felt guilty about his own success; at any
rate, he opened his wallet. With his money the reformers wrapped up a
package of proposals, worked their way into politics and set up an agency to investigate the community roots of accused criminals. They found a
number whose lengthy criminal records were proof that they came back
to court to take their medicine with disgusting regularity; as a result, they
persuaded so many judges that defendants didn't have to be held routinely
for six months until trial that the city saved money. The law was changed;
the reformers were held in high esteem; dozens of grants came in for other
worthy projects. But there was a price. Having proved what could be done,
they passed on the work to others who saw it merely as a job; the career
mentality took over. In a year detention rates were back to normal.

Despite visions of sunshine twelve months a year, I sail the letter from
Golden Fields across the room.

It must be clear by now why I fixed on Mr. Baker. We reformers, liberals,
planners, lawyers, journalists and educated types have met the opposition
and we are theirs. Despite our ideas and intentions, there is no more meat
than before in the stew. In fact, we have taken things to a point and then
made pretty much of a mess, changing ourselves far more than the rest.
Baker's stirrings were a chance to get on with it, perhaps the last chance before we become so immersed in talk about real-estate values that we don't
even have time to sign the checks. Here was no noble savage turning the
cheek, no Chairman Huey flaunting a gun, but (if I was right about the man)
self-transformation—a private self, a public transformation. Yeats put the
place where ladders start as the foul rag-and-bone shop of the heart.

On the phone from California my former student is cunning. He doesn't
tell me the temperature or report on his tennis game, doesn't pretend that
noisy educational radicalism still lives, and hardly wastes a word on the
budget fat he thinks I can turn into muscle. His only dig is to ask after the
health of the Soft Killer, but he trumps this with a sincere-sounding "We
need you." Apparently I can still persuade myself I am needed. Or is it just
the slush? "We need someone to tell us that it's all right to take a stand, a
consistent one—to have an ideology. You know, Jeremy, to be...political."

So I agree to have a look. At Golden Fields a week later I am passed from
faculty to search committee to student lounge to university president's office to lunch at the Quadrangle Club on mountains of fresh fruit and cottage cheese served by coeds, always smiling. It turns out that my ex-stu-
dent's idea of politics is to screw the central administration. "They pay their

French teachers with the money we earn by teaching large classes." The faculty also has an inferiority complex: no appointments at Harvard have been forthcoming. It is thought that I might remedy these ills by grantsmanship. To make it to the top they want centers, institutes, satellites. There is little said about what scholarly function they will perform, but the consensus is that having them will help put the school on the map. Here at last I find proof that lawyers are really different: no one else in California thinks so far ahead.

Between mouthfuls of fruit salad and sprouts, the search committee inquires gently where I stand, what I would do, what I think. They don't press and show less concern with what I say than with how I say it. They are looking for a unicorn—an East-facing workaholic who will let them keep sensible hours; they are trying to feel out whether I am an easygoing compulsive. Most disconcerting of all, I am asked repeatedly why I want to be dean. By the end of the day my neck hurts from ducking.

Meanwhile, in our nation's capital, I cling to my belief in the critical importance of statecraft and try to avoid noticing the furniture. The conversation is mostly about people or agencies.

"Max Appleseed is now at State."

"No, he's left already for Brookings."

"You know Max, don't you?"

It is my shame that I don't remember Max, and couldn't put the bite on him if I had to. Oh, well, maybe I knew his roommate. One of our early models coined a memorable phrase about my law school. He said the faculty was staffed by old Turks and young fogies. This is a variant: the young-boy network. Plugging into it, Sam attempts to bypass the swamp of twenty-year civil servants. In California they are plumbing my soul; in Washington, my resume. Absorbed by the role of prospective employee, it is easy to forget to ask myself whether I really want to carry a yoke.

Pieces of me have been left around the city. On my rounds I continually catch fleeting glimpses of what I was, am, could be. On the farm my spoor shows up in broken grass, tools abandoned, mounds of leaves, traces of lime. Here the trail is more difficult to spot; so many others have come the same way. Connie wants out on Tuesdays and Thursdays. On Mondays and Wednesdays she sees her shrink: she is undecided. He thinks New York is "where it's at." After so many loyal years of service to the cause, it is unkind and unfair that I think this is where his fees are at. I wince at the unannounced arrival of this thought, having complained to anyone who would listen about media failure to portray therapists as anything but venal, jargon-ridden, dull-witted. My experience was different; it was the best money I ever spent. This line isn't heard, even by me.

Fritz thinks a move from Big Town would be disastrous, but then Fritz has never been west of Lincoln Center; besides, wishing he were married to Connie, to his *idea* of Connie, he is hardly objective. Friends split into two camps: those who think executive responsibility as appealing as caring for the terminally ill, and those who see it as the route to power. Later the two camps converge, united in boredom. Do it, don't do it—only find something else to talk about. To which plea I urgently concur. Never bring it up, suffer in silence, perne in my gyre.

I do play it out to Rudy, since law school my brother, twin and partner in crime. He is busy writing a brief. With his thick skin, bushy brows and chunky neck, he looks like a teddy bear seated at a typewriter. Rudy's hobby is suing finance companies over usurious loans to spendthrift consumers. He badgers their lawyers with million-dollar civil-rights suits, even though skeptics believe the result of his efforts will be to raise the price of credit, keeping the gullible from purchasing the home freezer or Formica furniture of their choice.

As he sits poised over the machine, I turn him to stone.

He fights to eliminate himself from the equation. The good lawyer and the good friend at odds. He feels one must resist what the other should embrace. Does he counsel best who is removed from the picture? Is it just a question of role definition? The rule of thumb is that you get good advice from someone detached, but I no longer want friends who are detached or advice from people whose only role is to give it. If I was together about this thing and knew my mind, I would simply supply the information. But I have asked for help, though I can't imagine accepting it. I must want him to be part of the problem.

"You have to balance the costs and the benefits," Rudy replies.

A week later we meet with Herman Scalpino, the deputy corporation counsel. We are trying to get him to agree to the appointment of an inspector-general for the city's jails. Our prey is sympathetic, but he hasn't any money; in his department there is a freeze on paper clips. Herman also wants a court order to cover his ass against the inevitable slings and arrows. He wants to defend this case and then when he loses claim that he had to give us what we wanted. After all, he was just obeying the law, complying with destiny. But the law in this case is years away and we want relief now.

Herman is delivering a speech filled with explanations of why he must let the course of justice proceed: "I must remind you, it wasn't I who brought this suit." Behind him we see tugs scuttling up the river. The view is the only consolation of his job; because of it men have stayed for years in this unpainted office slum. The only control they have is a lordly perch above the madness below. On Herman's desk sit packets of square orange cards, the day's new claims against the body politic. He shuffles the pack and asks for sympathy. A cop is challenging the accuracy of an answer to a question on the desk sergeant's qualification exam. A schoolteacher insists she was forced by her principal to take a medical leave. Fourteen contractors and subcontractors are suing for cost overrides occasioned by a wrongful, negligent and otherwise tortious withholding of the necessary building permits. The Off-Track Betting Corporation, it is said, deters women from seeking executive employment. An old man fell in a pothole, breaking his hip while alighting from the Fourteenth Street crosstown. The federal government wants the return of a hundred million because somebody forgot to certify something and that somebody hasn't or won't because he is a holdover from the previous administration whom the mayor can't dump until the scoundrel's term of office expires.

"Listen, Herman," says Rudy, casting his line into the sea, "this case will cost you thousands in counsel fees. If we settle now, there'll be a waiver."

But Herman isn't biting. Four years hence some other fellow will have to explain that one, not him.

On our way out of the building, Rudy sees his first wife headed for Foley Square with a sharpie in tow, a rascal who can only be the defendant in a securities case. Her specialty is middle-class crooks suffering temporary insanity. This fellow looks frightened enough to qualify. The wind blows old newspapers in our faces. At the door to Hong Wah, our favorite Chinese restaurant, Rudy puts his knuckles in my back and pushes hard. "Jeremy," he says, "I don't want you to leave." He has made this effort at being personal from a position where I can't see his face, but at least he has followed his feelings. Feeding on incomparable broad noodles, we plot to go over Herman's head.

Dee refuses to talk about the subject of moving. She wants no democracy, no conferences with her parents. Her silence says, "This is your life. Leave me out of it."

My New York party trick, a sure-fire attention-getter, is to recall what I've seen where. Ray Bolger in *Where's Charley* at the St. James. Katharine Hepburn and William Prince in *As You Like It* at the Cort. Sammy Kaye, Martin and Lewis, and Nancy Walker on the stage of the old Capitol. Sneaking into the Garden to see Vince Boryla sink bombs from midcourt. I was once a spear carrier in *Aida* at the old Met. The Roxy, Paramount and Astor hotels are demolished, the Hole in the Wall and Stuyvesant Casino gone. If I missed these places, it would be easier to leave, but they have been placed in storage. They stay as I want them—old flats pulled to the rafters. The wrecker's ball enhances the difficulty and brings gasps from the uninitiated. Even Dee likes to hear that I petted in the balcony of what is now a supermarket while Dick Powell and June Allyson played in *The Reformer and the Redhead*. Connie's favorite double bill is *Wild for Kicks* and *Nudism Today*, held over for months at the World. I saw De Sica's *Bicycle Thief* there in 1950.

Arrangements

THERE ARE times when to distract me from my daily balancing act I wish Connie would take a lover. Perhaps she already has and I don't know it. That marks the biggest change—not that she might have or that occasionally I want her to, but that I wouldn't know it. "Look," I say, "man is a player, but in the city we don't have the space or time enough for outdoor sports, so we have affairs. That's what we do—secret affairs. Polygamy is out. Keeping a mistress is burdensome. Go have yours. You don't need my permission." The tears flow, covering the scorn. But I am steadfast in the right. If an edict came down from the seat of power banning these intimate moments caught on the run, the center really would not hold. After raging at our kids and looking for a good war, we would take to the streets, mobs of would-be lovers blindly vandalizing midtown. And the higher you go, the deeper the need to escape. If you doubt it, look at the recent history of the Presidency.

Annie, my own favorite ex-lover, nagged me into taking her out to the Island to have a look at my old neighborhood. Fire had destroyed the house of my childhood, now replaced by a boxy builder's special. The boardwalk was fringed with old-age homes. My public school had been torn down, and the penny arcade was a grimy variety store where everything cost sixty-nine cents. On the empty lots near the ocean the city had built high-rise public housing. Only the Orthodox temple looked unchanged, though the window I broke playing stick ball was no longer cracked. The kids had scattered as worshipers poured out of the building sure that a pogrom was in progress, but I stood my ground. The first to arrive, young men in their early twenties wearing tight-fitting suits, wool knitted ties, trimmed beards and broad-rimmed, felt-banded hats, came at me with fists stiffly held like hammers. No wonder the Germans could kill them, I thought, simply pointing in explanation at the broom handle, secure in my American understanding of innocence.

They failed to strike but gripped me hard and hustled me into the shul to await the arrival of two Irish cops. The broken minyan chattered like hungry starlings in a tree. Old men in black silk peered through the circle that formed around the pew in which I was tossed, eager to see the storm trooper. It never occurred to me that I might be harmed. This was my country; they must be here on sufferance. I finally put an end to it merely by saying, "I am Jewish." They stopped in mid-chirp. I retrieved the pink rubber ball everyone called a "spaldeen," though it was manufactured by the Spalding Company of Chicopee, Massachusetts, and held it aloft like an orb. This told the cops their business was over; they ordered me to beat it.

Annie enjoys stories of my childhood but tries not to show it. Her struggle is to mask exuberance. She has taken to hiding the curves of her body beneath long black skirts, ties, cowls, heavy Mexican jackets. At work she must suppress her feelings.

"This memo is hysterical," says her bureau chief, complaining mainly about its enthusiasm.

"All right, all right, I'll do it over." Screwed up again, she thinks. Too blunt. "But we're doing nothing, absolutely nothing, about the juvenile detention facilities in this city. Children are treated worse now than when they used to slave fourteen hours a day in the mills."

Annie lives with her son Josh in one of the highest crime areas of the city, in a house that is continually burgled. Once in the middle of the night two men tried to break in by using a crowbar on the basement door. She called the police and her upstairs tenant, locked herself in Josh's bedroom and waited until the tenant's shouts scared them away. The police never came. In the morning she found the huge iron door to the basement fluttering flaglike on its hinges. Shaking, she put water on for coffee, then stood under the shower for twenty minutes. Slowly, feeling came back into her body. I still felt close enough to Annie so that I could see the details as she told the story. She dressed in front of the mirror, brushing her long yellow hair, the only person with such hair that she knew in New York, and for the third time in a month decided that—honorary Jew or not—this time she would move out of the city. She saw the excessive breasts that had embarrassed her so often as a teenager, and remembered the catcalls from the park one night a week earlier as she walked home from a movie. She had kept on walking, unwilling to acknowledge that they were meant for her. Suddenly the tears came, and she flung herself on the brass bed, pounding it with her fists. In the afternoon she was sarcastic to a foundation program officer who had honestly reported that there was very little chance of a grant. He hadn't known what to make of it, hadn't recognized it for what it was. Foundation people see all kinds. Some con, some are even hostile, most cultivate sincerity, but no one is sarcastic to the Ford Foundation.

Annie's husband, Mort, lives in the same neighborhood a few streets away. They have an arrangement. He has his own apartment because he doesn't want her crowding him. They talk often, usually when they hit an empty space—the black-hole syndrome is her name for it. He calls when the woman he sees is out of town. She calls about Josh or if something goes wrong with the house—he can do plumbing and electrical work—or when her job has let her down by not being demanding enough to send her home exhausted. Or on Sunday morning, unless one of the two men she sleeps with has stayed over; since they're both married, she usually faces the *Times* alone.

Mort is too handsome for his own good, and has never known a time when there wasn't someone to make his bed. He is a sociologist who caused a stir two years ago with a study of health-care delivery systems by demonstrating, with an impressive amount of empirical research, how federal money produced far more surgery than was prudent simply because of the profit motive built into the subsidy. The media had a field day, and one district attorney promised an investigation. Most striking to the newspaper-reading public were several documented cases of elderly people put to the knife for no reason more apparent than the desire of the surgeons to collect a government fee. A serious intellectual with strong radical views, Mort is much in demand as an adviser to insurgent politicians, consultant to legislative committees with a license to muckrake for a season, campus lecturer. The care and feeding of his wife and child imply a warmth that for him is both politically regressive and in short supply; Annie says they split because she doesn't want a roommate.

Keeping her feelings manageable makes her in turn aggressive, harsh, gregarious, scattered, and then sad, composed, maudlin, shy, deferential. Like the woman in Mary's fragment of a novel, for a long time she has felt that if the mind is a place—a house, she supposes—there are rooms where men make the difference and drop the cues. Armed with this insight, she decided to get tough with herself and became a furious worker, challenging lawyer and effective money raiser.

Her father was a Romanist, a man so immersed in the first century that his transaction with his own time had a remarkable gentleness. His ambitions were vast but narrow. He loved his two sons but doted on his eldest daughter. Her mother was a housewife: "There is no other word to describe her," Annie says sadly. "My problem has always been," she explained to her therapist, "that the mother in me won't go away." She had been programmed to be an exceptional one, but at college had done very well and become entangled with big, powerful, ambitious men. Once snared, she stopped thinking; she became vapid, vacuous, cowlike, passive—a thing. When this mood set in (she always knew its arrival because she had trouble getting up in the morning), either she or they lost interest. Talking about this subject makes her irritable and bored. One, then the other, in sequence.

"I should give it all up and write, I should have another baby, I should see my shrink more. Oh, shit, shit, shit." I've taken her to my favorite bar for this outburst. Tucked away in an old hotel now become residential, there are always peanuts on the tables, it is never crowded, and the waiters always act as if I'm their honored guest. Except for city government, most of the good things in New York are run at a loss.

"I don't get along with men. Maybe it's the size of my vagina. Now, there's an issue no one talks about; I've yet to see an article touting a cure, but a loose fit causes more divorce than adultery."

"Be patient. *New York* magazine will get to it."

"Anyway, I went out with a guy last week. A quiet mood, everything was swell. We talked about California. Last night I saw him again. We went downtown to visit Susan and Kit at the loft to look at her paintings. Too big to sell, but exciting stuff. Then I made a big mistake. We went out for dinner with some friends of theirs, and I just forgot him. I wasn't nasty; I just forgot I was his. I talked to everybody else and interrupted him. I didn't follow the deference patterns he'd learned at Porkchop, Lambchop and Hambone. And don't think you're any different."

Out of her purse come phone book, diary, a tortoiseshell hairbrush, two pens and a list. She slips down in the booth and studies her week, crossing off and adding, then on a fresh piece of paper makes a new list.

The love between us is lost, but more than enough intimacy remains. Annie and I are nursing each other as well as our drinks, trying to stuff the day in a file drawer and lock the cabinet so we can forget it. The judge is leaning on us to work out our differences with the lawyers for the newspaper. Of eighty-five interrogatories we have propounded, they've answered six satisfactorily; all the rest is garbage. Their hiring and promotion patterns are still covered with gauze. They claim privilege or attach the wrong documents or just blather at us. Three hours of haggling has us nowhere. They just can't find enough qualified blacks and women, blah, blah, blah.

Annie has talked common sense and turned salty when they don't buy it. She has forgotten that their meter is running. It will take us several more trips to Foley Square before they give in. She is particularly testy about Armand Wolfe, my classmate from law school, who always looks at me for a reply. "It's not that you're impatient," she says, in a mood turned as sharply as city streets turn corners. "With you, it's the assumption that you have to do something, that you're responsible for what happens." Once, lying flat on her bed she insisted on undressing me, a two-hour operation punctuated by shoptalk. After a good lick I came within seconds, laughing, panting, light from the lifted weight.

While we haggle, Armand treats us to some lawyer's rhetoric.

"Let me give it to you in one of those proverbial nutshells," he says. "They dump their crap on you, and the man—or woman, naturally, of course, yes—who carries the crap wears the crown. Listen, don't get me wrong, but a little inequality is a good thing. No one is going to put up with first-year law school or listen to lawyer's language or read the fine print unless you pay them off with prestige, dominance and a fat check every few weeks. Sure, the thing has come to feed on itself. Get it? Disputes mean more lawyers and more lawyers mean more disputes. But the real ripoff, after all, is that I am the one who draws the line. I get to tell people what they can do and can't, what is legal and illegal, and for most of them that gets confused with what is right and wrong. And I get to do it vicariously, without risk; I am only serving my client, toots."

This is Armand's heavy-handed way of showing off his machismo for Annie's benefit. But the tough and worldly talk is defeated by his neatness. The only distinguishing feature of the Wall Street lawyers I know is their neatness. At Good Works and at the clinic we have court suits. Annie and Clare have court pants suits, but we are never really neat, never sleek. Dee is disgusted that her father wears faded trousers and gets his hair cut every three months; that the gray hasn't won the war. The taxi driver who took me uptown to school last week asked if I was a teacher or a student.

Armand pulls this crap for Annie's benefit, but he hopes I won't take it as a sly putdown. If riled, I might tell her he was only twelfth in his class. These things count in the legal world. At a law school of the first rank, which will remain nameless to protect the guilty, they recently refused a teaching appointment to a man in his fifties who had been serving with distinction in Washington when most of the faculty were still mastering boxball. He was an expert in one of those crannies of corporate finance that curriculum committees usually love, but his grades right after the Second World War were only so-so. And in Armand's set they still talk about who pulled four A's—now called Excellents—the first semester. The best students were distinguished from the herd the way National Football League first-round draft choices are separated from the rest.

I reply in kind. "Everything you say about the bar is true, and as you well know a week's digging would turn up enough fertilizer to solve India's food problem for a decade. But you're missing why we are so necessary. People don't talk to each other. That's why everything has to be covered in unintelligible regulations, written down in rococo contracts and stored in library warehouses. There is no oral tradition. They will talk sometimes in their own trades or offices, but once you get them away from the safe and familiar they need lawyers. We are bringing Esperanto to the Tower of Babel. Did you read about the fellow in upstate New York who offered free buffalo to an Indian tribe if the members would let his herd graze on tribal lands? He prepared a written contract but the Indians had no faith in anything scribbled by a white man; they came back carrying a cowskin on which they had painted pictures of the bargain. Can you imagine what they'd do with that at Lambchop, Hambone?"

Armand has grown rich from disasters. When a jumbo jet goes down anywhere in the world, widows and orphans make their way to the nearest law office. Few of these attorneys know the first thing about suing Boeing, a conglomerate of insurance carriers and an airline. They do know a good thing, however, so these locals contact Armand or one of the other Wall Street octopi that specialize in plane crashes and sell him the case for a slice of the recovery. Armand says there's always a settlement because none of these planes goes down without somebody having screwed up. The dead passengers certainly didn't cause the crash. His job is to make a big enough fuss over the case to justify his fee. He and his boys paper everything: they examine the people who made the plane, the controllers who tracked the flight, the weatherman who failed to predict a rainstorm. Meanwhile, the defense lawyers have to sell *their* bill of goods to the insurance companies. They file their own motions, run background checks on the victims, dispute the expected jury recoveries and argue about the proper court in which to try the case. Eventually the defense lawyers show their clients the neatly bound booklet Armand has prepared on all the dead passengers, listing the actuarials plus their job prospects if they'd survived to a ripe old age, and the woeful state of their now indigent dependents. The lawyers prepare an opinion that a jury will slap a million-dollar-a-head judgment on the companies because they know that Armand can be bought off for seven hundred and fifty thousand. When they bring the case in for three-quarters of a million, the businessmen think the lawyers are heroes.

This and a lot more like it has soured me on the profession, makes me wish I didn't have a lawyer's talent for shaving points and plucking people. Inertia—and my unshakable habit of inducing dependence in myself and others—keeps me at it—though there is one lawyer's trait that deflates my cynicism and dignifies our presence on this earth. I mean the tools to expose and explode fallacy in public. Not many of us get to do it. Most of our time is spent conjuring and very little in showing the audience how to do the tricks. It's sad that an attorney can carry a license for a lifetime without ever encountering the opportunity to reverse opinion, change belief or move a crowd when it matters. But there are those lucky few who make the most of their chances; they serve for the rest of us, and keep the spirit alive waiting to be grasped in every courtroom.

With his uncanny skill at mounting a weekly parade of witness-stand confessions to murder, Perry Mason has made this phenomenon available to millions. That is why he is the most influential law teacher in America. In fact, Raymond Burr, the actor whose identity is now inseparable from Mason's, has sent me so many students that I feel obliged to watch as many of his grainy, black-and-white reruns as I can. Despite the absurd plotting he must work with, Burr is successful because he understands the basic similarity between lawyering and acting. In both, mastery of a script frees one to be unpredictable and to get past the words to the sense. Burr, of course, has an ally in the camera that is not available to us journeymen. Whenever he scores a point with the jury by turning from a witness in total disbelief, the director immediately gives the viewer a close-up of the guilty party. Under this enlarged scrutiny no face can avoid self-betrayal.

In the real life of the law, the spaces are far too generous, and it is a rarity even for the great ones—all of whom are superb actors—to encounter drama so high that it fixes the eye to every twitch. A courtroom is simply too big a box. Occasionally we manage to produce the right lawyer to bend history's otherwise languid arc, someone who provokes all but the most biased to display falsehood and shed self-interest. In those moments when the shoddy falls I am proud I wear the same tie: Welch toppling McCarthy with a finger; Biko's captors exposed as thugs not because we assumed it from the start but because now we have proof; Bryan trapped by Darrow's relentless logic. Anyone fortunate enough to observe this art practiced in the flesh will not soon forget the experience. The tide shifts, fear and doubt ebb; for a while we have our certainty. This may sound more than a trifle romantic, fit only for a bar association speech on Law Day, but for me the skill that makes it possible is genius. It ties craft to a higher purpose; it keeps me at my desk.

Against the evidence, I still feel I could have done something else with my life, though when I had the opportunity I didn't take it. Israel was my frontier, the source of the Nile, the emotional equivalent of Tombstone, Dodge City, the Alamo.

The weekend after I lost my job with a Jerusalem newspaper I helped my friend Seth move his things to a kibbutz in the Galilee. On the trip back to the city the police stopped my bus and wounded an Arab they'd been

searching for. I never found out why they wanted him. I didn't reach the
hostel in Jerusalem until midnight, after my new roommate was asleep.
When I awoke the next morning, he was sitting at the end of the other
bed, tying the laces of heavy paratrooper boots. He wore a jumper's beret
but was older than most Israeli soldiers. He moved to the basin, then realized he was being watched and wheeled around as if surprised by a Bedouin
ambush. All he said was "Shalom." On his way out, he paused and lit a cigarette. "American?"

"Right."

"Sporting around or serious?"

"Just to see."

"You are a student?"

A reflexive yes, but I wasn't anymore, and had yet to find a new category.

The trooper hitched his trousers and set his cap. "I'll give you some advice. The Americans think they are safe, but I know different. It is only a
matter of time before you have your Hitler, before you have to stop play-
acting that you're Jewish. Why aren't you staying in Israel? You have your
McCarthys, your racists. It's only a matter of time. Listen here, in the war
the Palestinians were commanded by an Arab named Salameh who was a
major in the German army. They dropped him in Jericho in 1944. You get
my meaning?"

Holbrook, the man whose approval I needed, looked as if he'd been carefully lifted off the flat Indiana landscape with a spatula and expertly placed
in the small office off the main lobby of the Jerusalem YMCA. He talked in
the friendly, fatherly way of a professional Christian, but he wasn't hood-
winked by me. Apparently I was not the first with this request. He showed
no interest in hearing a definition of the Trinity or probing whether my
parents really were Christian Scientists.

"Things have been quiet over there, but Easter weekend is another matter. Please be discreet. And don't stray into no man's land, especially around
Har Zion. There are snipers—fanatics."

He signed the papers that the embassy said would allow me to enter
Jordan by the Mandelbaum Gate on Good Friday morning and return on
Easter Sunday.

The next morning I walked through the Meah Sheareem, past still-glow-
ing embers of the communal bonfire where zealots burn their bread before
Passover. The Israelis waved me through with a glance at my papers. On
the Jordanian side the guards were all mustached, imitations of their king.
I crossed with an American who was living on a kibbutz in the Negev, a
round, cheerful girl named Roberta. She *was* a Christian Scientist and had

come to Israel, as I had, because it was getting cold in Greece. As we walked, she gave me a careful rundown of the national characteristics of European motorists, based roughly on the amount of time it took them to reach for her bush. We found a hotel outside the gates. An Arab showed us a window-less shed that had been fitted out for tourists: a washstand, two single beds and a crucifix. The walls were the blue of a Spanish mackerel to keep off the evil eye. Nondenominational. We dumped our gear, and she headed for the Mount of Olives.

Inside the walls the narrow stone streets of the Old City were jammed with pilgrims—ascetic Scandinavians, porky Germans, Greek monks, a party of Lebanese Christians. The tourists pressed toward a gate framing an immense wooden cross. The crowd hushed. In a language I could not place a man dressed in a Roman tunic and helmet shouted to a comrade. They were whipping Jesus. As the lash cut the air, the procession surged forward and pushed me into a square covered with trinket tables—plastic crosses, candles, panda bears and dioramas of the Crucifixion. Above the din I heard the groaning of Our Savior and the angry voices of the Romans.

They marched to another station of the cross, the crowd following, laughing, attempting to get a glimpse of the scene, but the street was nar-row and crooked. At the next stop the hushing of the audience moved like a wave. The Roman shouted, Jesus was flogged, the players grunted at the twang of the whip, the crowd sighed. Then I heard a chant off to the right where another narrow alley crossed the Via Dolorosa. Three young Arabs, almost children, with kaffiyehs framing their faces, emerged from the alley. They used their elbows to clear the way; behind them were youths waving fists to a chant.

"Hussein, Hussein."

"Nas-ser, Nas-ser, Nas-ser."

In the center of the group, held aloft in corrugated metal frames, were poster-size photographs of the two leaders torn from a newspaper. The demonstrators passed through the parting crowd, shaking fists in cadence. I huddled against the stones, pushed back by the milling tourists.

"Hussein, Nas-ser. Hussein, Nas-ser."

A soldier appeared, shouted to the icon carriers and waved them back with his rifle. The tourists turned and aimed their cameras.

A platoon of soldiers worked through the crowd, cleaving tourists and demonstrators. One of the teenage boys gave them the finger as they passed. "Nas-ser, Nas-ser." A blond-bearded Scandinavian in a white suit raised his arms high above his head and clicked. The chant mingled with the sound of the whip. At first the soldiers stood together, holding their sticks in two hands parallel to the ground, pushing the marchers back toward the neck of the alley. The two groups froze like this for an instant, equally balanced and thus immobile. An officer in starched brown climbed the stone steps of a church and shouted orders in Arabic. The tourists pressed against the walls on the far side of the tiny square. The Scandinavian worked his camera, his eyes gleaming. Blood on the face of one of the children broke the line. Like swarming sharks, the soldiers suddenly attacked in frenzy. They grabbed the front line, three and four to one, tripping the young men with their sticks, stomping and kicking, until the whimpers of the demonstrators were louder than the heavy breathing of the soldiers. Others dashed down the alley—screaming Technicolor Indians—tearing the posters from their frames. When it was over, I felt too weak to stand. I realized that I had not moved and had never felt threatened, but my clothes were wet. In five minutes there was nothing left but dark stains on the paving. In the glittering sun of a cloudless day I trembled. The procession stumbled on to another station of the cross.

In the afternoon I confronted the typical problem of unlearned American Jews visiting the then Arab-controlled Old City—how to find Ha Kotel, the Wailing Wall. Before crossing the border I consulted several Israelis who had been born or brought up in Jerusalem before partition. One of them, Ezra, the janitor at the hostel, in turn expressed astonishment, disbelief and finally hostility when I told him about crossing for Easter. A man used to seeing well-fed young people, most of them Americans, he was jealous of my approach to the Holy of the Holies, the lingering of the spirit. Later he forgave me when I presented him with a picture of the Wall. He'd been in the Old City in 1948 when an Arab mine blew up the water pipes supplying the Jewish quarter. There were fifteen hundred Jews behind sandbags, barbed wire, roadblocks and sand-filled tar barrels. Huddled on sacred ground, they refused to leave. Every two weeks the British ferried supplies into the quarter in an armed convoy. Ezra smuggled guns in through tunnels dug beneath a monastery. The wadi he crossed under sentry fire is clearly visible from the cocktail lounge of the King David Hotel.

Behind the Dome of the Rock was a gate leading to a rabbit warren of little streets. At one turning a fat woman with a face the color of amontillado sat on a chair in a doorway, talking to a child. When the woman nodded, I took it as a sign. The sun cast shadows across the narrow street. Only my face was warm. Down an alley I saw the huge stones. I remembered pictures of black-gowned old men facing the Wall. To get there I walked to the end of the street and turned a corner. Again I trembled, but no one was there, the narrow space between the Wall and the houses was empty. I looked up and down, and wiped away the sweat.

To a child of skyscrapers, the Wall was not high. The blocks of stone were shorter than girders and softened by improbable bushes leaning out like gargoyles. But the density of the rock, its scale in comparison to the hovels that surrounded it, caught me in a dream fashioned by De Chirico. There was absolute silence. I leaned against the Wall and murmured the prayer over wine, the only one I knew.

To deal with the fear I walked down the alley, first retracing my path, then hopelessly lost. No one was about. The houses were identical, as if cut from the same block of stone, and shut tight against the heat. By the time I stumbled onto the roadway that unsuccessfully attempted to circle a city cut in two, I was certain I'd never get out. I almost fell upon a group of Arab children playing in the dust. When they saw the tall bearded figure stagger out where the squat buildings met the street, they ran off screaming. Even I could understand that they used the Arabic word for Jew.

Connie says there are three levels of experience. The primary experience is the real thing—whatever that is. The secondary experience is the artistic or journalistic representation of life, whether realistically or romantically portrayed. The third level—and this is the one that really interests her and makes her frown with disapproval—is the vicarious. The vicarious is not supposed to be the real thing or its artistic representation, but rather a substitute trivialized by sentimentality and made more palatable by misrepresentation. The positive is enhanced, the negative disregarded. Things are made more colorful, up-to-date, more manageable in scale. A few years after I left, the Israelis began naming tourist attractions after the characters in Exodus. So many Americans have asked the Dutch about Pieter, the boy who put his finger in the dyke in *Hans Brinker, or The Silver Skates*, that a statue has been put up commemorating his birthplace. The *Times* reliably reports that there was no Pieter, and that the Dutch words used by the German-American lady who wrote the book were misspelled German. The statue in Spaarndam was a simple business decision. Disneyland must be the ultimate expression of the genre. There is nothing of this kind in Manhattan; no one could suspend disbelief.

The archaeological expedition that I joined assembled in the courtyard of an army post, the tawny baked earth as hard and impenetrable as concrete. The soldiers milled about and flirted with the girls. A deeply tanned sabra talked with his hands to an Austrian blonde who spoke no Hebrew. Dressed in white pants, a red jersey and a blue scarf, holding a hand to shade skin the color of mashed potatoes, she could have been standing on a dock waiting to board a sloop for a day of sailing. The plum hands of the sabra rose and fell in front of a ginger mustache in what I read as the preliminaries of a mating ritual. So sharp was the contrast, enhanced by the vivid light of the desert morning, that the crew sprawled on its dunnage to watch. I was still to notice Connie amidst the duffles and sacks.

I suppose this splinter of memory is the real thing, but even as I took it in, my mind played with it; I wondered what would become of these two in the weeks ahead, and even fantasized two sets of astonished and disapproving parents. Hers voted for Hitler; his reached the docks at Trieste days before they sealed the border. Never again, to be sure, but our tendency to forget is salvation as well as curse.

Hesh, the army captain, counted and re-counted the mess of packs, the canteens dangling from their straps, cartons of evaporated milk, boxes of white bread and tinned beans. Porath, the leader, joined him, dressed like a common soldier; his fatigues had no marking, and only the pipe he filled and refilled seemed to symbolize that at Suez he wore a general's star. The square knitted cap perched on his head barely hid his baldness from the sun. It was nine o'clock and already too hot to move.

Trucks lurched into the yard and we climbed up, stuffing our gear between the benches. They were open to the sun, but movement stirred a slight breeze. Porath rode in the lead jeep, but after the first rest stop, where a track cut across the desert toward the Dead Sea, he came to us and stood swaying, his back against the cab. We were searching for traces of Jews who rebelled against the Romans in the second century. He told us they chose to die rather than surrender. We leaned forward to hear over the motor, and lay on the bags stacked in the well. We would, he said, be close enough to the border to worry about infiltrators.

I was still in a daze from the night before. After hitching from Jerusalem to Beersheba, I found the Carpe Diem. It was early, the bar still closed, but I wandered in anyway and stretched out under a green and white umbrella, a fugitive from some Left Bank café. I peeled open a tin of sardines, sliced bread with a pocketknife, watched the sun die over the desert, killed the dregs of the sweet Carmel wine in the canteen and huddled in my jacket to keep out the cold.

Before I saw Baba, the woman who ran the place, I heard her talking to the children in English and tried with my clumsy Hebrew to catch the gist of her instructions to an elderly woman. A shower gurgled from the far end of the square building across the yard. The wine made me drowsy, and I yawned beneath the quilting. Seth, who had told me Baba would let me stay overnight, described her as a small, quick woman with brown hair, a woman of a certain age, used but not abused. Before coming to Israel, Seth had been a schoolteacher in Great Neck. On Yom Kippur he saw a group of men wearing dark suits and sneakers standing in front of a Brooklyn synagogue. He stopped and asked about the sneakers. The explanation— something about not wearing hides from living things—failed to satisfy him, and he entered the temple. A man was saying the prayer for the dead. He had thought the Day of Atonement was concerned with guilt. After the service, he felt he had talked to God about the future. He began to study Hebrew, refused pork and shellfish, quit his job, left his wife.

Baba came to the umbrella as if we had an appointment, pulled up an iron café chair and began to smoke. "Here for the expedition?" she asked, but added without waiting for an answer, "You are welcome to sleep in the bar." The children joined us and arranged themselves around their mother like petals. "Say hello to Mr. American from..."

"New York."

Stacey, Baba's husband, ambled across the yard, his hand distractedly rubbing the back of his neck. He was a heavy man turning to fat, immense biceps and round shoulders showing through a red-checked short-sleeved shirt; a squat nose sat between cheeks rough as a file.

According to Seth, who lived at the Carpe Diem for a month, Stacey was an early human-potential-movement guru, one of the first to settle near Big Sur and one of the first to leave. He had come to Israel shortly after the Suez invasion and used his James Jones-Hemingway looks to wangle a combat assignment. After taking a Czech-made, Egyptian-fired bullet in the abdomen, he met Baba and opened a bar in Jaffa where he had trouble with the police over his unwillingness to make the usual payments. They had moved to the edge of the Negev's emptiness and found this abandoned Arab house. Stacey rebuilt it with stones that he carried from the desert on his back, and now the Carpe Diem was a place where every Israeli on the road to Elath had to stop for a drink; even the Tourist Authority had begun to tout it. Stacey served all comers and the bar had remained unchanged, but Seth wondered how much longer he could put up with this sort of success. They were, as Seth said, an improbable couple.

Stacey shuffled into the bar with a wave in our direction. "To bed, Pietro, Tia, to bed." The little boy gave his mother a malicious grin, the face of a child testing a boundary, and ran off to follow his father, all the while looking back, taking her measure. She lit another cigarette.

"And how is Seth?" she asked.

"Trying to sink in roots. He has joined a kibbutz near Belt Sha'an but doesn't know whether to stay in Israel or go home. His religious revival is having trouble surviving the Holy Land. He finds it a place like any other."

She held the smoke in her lungs as if nicotine were good for her. "He won't last."

"I don't know," I said, as if defending my friend. "He still talks seriously."

"Wait until summer, when the conversation begins to smell like the cow shit they'll give him to shovel."

I was about to say she sounded bitter, but this had been said evenly, with so little feeling about the edges, that I hesitated. She smiled the cat smile of a compact and beautiful French woman, a smile bred to tease and please. A butterfly.

"The Americans who stay either have come to a dead end or never had anywhere to go in the first place. Americans are more suited to worshiping from afar; we are stashed away just in case they need us, a numbered account in a Swiss bank. It's not strange for a country of immigrants and refugees that they don't like being last off the boat. Seth still believes in undertakings and possibilities; I didn't come until I'd given up on Paris."

"How was that?"

She was quiet and gave me an appraising look, the first point of contact. Was I a good enough catch to keep? "Of course," Seth had said, "Stacey is so tanked most of the time that it's difficult to know what's going on in his head. I have no idea what holds them together—they barely speak—but it's quite clear she makes up her own mind about the men in her life."

"Have you ever heard of *Combat*?"

"Camus' paper? During the Resistance, wasn't it?"

"Journalism is a joke, except perhaps in wartime—a joke I played on myself to think I had influence."

The lights came on, filling the dusky yard with a reddish glow. A string of tiny bulbs had been strung from the roof of the bar to a post at the side of the garden—red, green and blue, flickering Christmas lights. In the distance we heard a jazz flute. Thoughts crowded in and my head began to ache; too many were trying to force themselves on my consciousness. I'd been moving from place to place like this for a year, sleeping where the driver of the car dropped me, following the traveler in the next seat, taking what work I could find. In return for simply being there, like a paperback book left behind in a hotel room, people picked me up, took care of me, insisted that I use the extra bed, showed me the city and bought me expensive dinners.

Seth said I looked available. "You're easy to talk to and don't seem to care where you go next." I didn't deny it, but my patrons put as much into me as

I put into them: though the American dream may have been dying at home, it was alive and well east of Paris. But Baba didn't look as if she was going anywhere; she seemed bound to this yard floating in the desert.

The bar was plastered to look like a cave, a movie-set bistro. Candles flickered from plates and wax-crusted wine bottles. The walls were painted with credible trompe l'oeils copied from a guide book to Versailles. Booths were enveloped by undulating plaster, fissures of privacy. I drank Turkish coffee from an espresso machine that Stacey had rigged to the generator. Hash was restricted to the courtyard; the smokers sauntered outside, gleaming fireflies.

Stacey watched his world from a stool behind the bar, sitting in front of a mirror that broke the candlelight into little diamonds. When he moved to pour a drink or pull the lever that sent boiling water over the coffee beans, it was with the regal air of a working drunk. In conversation he was taciturn and ungiving.

Baba moved from table to table, talking with the American oil riggers from wells the Israelis were sinking near the Sinai, soldiers on leave, a group of kibbutzniks heading to the Red Sea, while I tried to get Stacey to talk about his new Italian coffee maker. Baba couldn't know everybody, but she acted as if she must touch each traveler before he disappeared into the night. When she heard a snatch of my labored conversation with Stacey, she joined us. "Your friend is a puppy dog, but you are a...hawk. Why do you go to dig? Are you an archaeologist?"

"I lost my job two weeks ago when an editor of the Jerusalem *Post* decided that a friend of his was a better proofreader."

"And was he?"

"Yes, she was. So I thought some time in the desert looking for scrolls would keep me out of trouble. Porath needs volunteers."

"Trouble."

She laughed. Stacey said nothing.

I was still eager to hear about wartime Paris. "Seth tells me you've had an interesting life and can be persuaded to tell the story if someone asks nicely."

"Well, which story do you want?" The coquette was now in full bloom. "I have many."

Stacey rocked on his stool, as silent and abstracted as a man watching a chess match.

"Why the Carpe Diem?"

"Easy. Stacey is from California, and Beersheba has more than a little of the Wild West about it. You see the short fellow with the Levis? When he drinks too much, he explodes. Stacey has had to throw him out before."

I gazed at a face that reminded me of a redheaded scat-back I once tackled in a scrimmage with the varsity. He went down so easily that for weeks I wondered why I wasn't starting in his place. "He looks friendly enough."

"That's part of the problem. Alcohol tells him to believe that my husband is his chum. Stacey isn't interested, so they argue."

I looked at Stacey, hoping to draw him into the conversation, but he merely stared back. I turned away, embarrassed. Baba pretended not to notice.

"Let's suppose I were doing a magazine piece on the bar—the sort of thing that brings you wealthy travelers to drink the spirit of the new land and sup on legends." If Stacey refused to be polite, I would be sarcastic. "What do I say?"

"You need a good lead."

"That's right."

"Start with a person. That's the American formula. I've been to America."

"Where?"

"Washington. California."

"And New York?"

"Only the airport. I have my limits."

"How about this: 'Baba yawns when visitors question her about the name of her Beersheba cafe, located on the edge of Israel's teeming city in the desert. She has been asked the question so often in the three years the cafe has existed that she has a pat answer. She tells them that after her experience in the French Resistance and her husband's role in the 1956 war with Egypt they had to seize the opportunity to die in bed. Baba is a charming French woman who with her American husband owns the popular café, a gathering place for Israeli artists and intellectuals, as well as local miners and kibbutzniks.'"

"Pretty good."

"Tell me," Stacey said, "why do you assume you're so superior?"

It was a stern and disconcerting rebuke, though put in the manner of a researcher who had studied a slide, digested its contents and formulated a hypothesis. He had been watching me.

"Am I that obvious?"

Answering a question with a question did not please him. He moved down the bar to pour iced vodka for two customers.

"It was this way all the time with Seth." Baba looked concerned. "Next he'll be reading your palm."

When Stacey returned, he unloaded his bile. "I get a sense of smugness from you, as if you're fucking the world and everyone should watch. Of course, you've got opportunities and half the people you meet in this country, especially the women, can smell it; they're aware they live in No-wheresville, something like Queens, where their only prospect is a flat with a terrace to hang out the laundry. But they only know you from the movies. Don't take it personally."

"You're saying that I trade on my passport?" I felt alone and vulnerable.

"Right, though I doubt you're daring enough to do it maliciously."

"How would you know?"

"Like the top sergeant says, 'I seen 'em come, seen 'em go.'"

"What makes you think Americans are so loved?"

"Envied and despised both. Envied for our golden goodies, for acting as if we deserved them when they just came to us because of where we popped out of the womb. Despised because we promote it and spread the news. This country survives on U.S. bond drives, French airplane parts and German reparations."

"So we're not alone."

"Tweedledum and Tweedledee."

"Leave him be, Stacey."

"Just trying to be helpful, my sweet. This one has the attitude of a young man on the make, straight from Stendhal. He probably doesn't realize that half of Tel Aviv wishes the boat that brought them here had landed instead at Miami Beach."

"I'm not offended."

"Of course not. How could you be? You'll go back to prospects, bossdom. You aren't stuck here. Just remember Uncle Stacey's words of wisdom: they want to get close to what they think they should have, and don't."

"You dish this out, but what about yourself?"

"Me? I'm just a jolly alcoholic who likes to keep close to his sauce. A disillusioned barkeep. Baba will tell you. She has a story memorized."

Baba turned back to the room—whether away from the boredom of a scene she had viewed before or private torment, I could not tell. Stacey slapped my shoulder to say no hard feelings and drifted down the bar. I knew his anger wasn't meant for me; nevertheless, I felt he'd got the picture right, more or less. Watching people pass through from city to desert must have sharpened his eye.

The Carpe Diem thinned out. Several couples danced to mournful Arab music. I dozed in a corner booth until the red-haired scatback threw a bottle. A tray stacked with glasses crashed to the tile floor. Two soldiers held him for Stacey; he landed solid blows to the stomach and head before dumping the twisted body in the unpaved street outside the gate. Later Baba slipped into my sleeping bag, but she shook her head when I tried to talk. In the morning she was gone; I never did learn about Camus and the Resistance.

By the Dead Sea I was deep in my private drama of self-importance. At first I chalked it up to unaccustomed guard duty near hostile territory, walking the perimeter of the camp on a three-hour watch with the unfamiliar weight of a loaded submachine gun in my hands, a model that the Israelis exported in quantity to the West German army. It took no great military experience to see that we were exposed to forays from raiders who might easily slip across the unguarded border from Jordan, reach our camp in less than an hour and return unmolested across the Judean Hills.

Increasingly, violence had crossed my path: the Arab on the bus, the paratrooper's warning, police fury against the Easter demonstrators, the man with the bottle, this merciless weapon. But only words had been directed at me; there was no reason, I told myself, to be anxious. Fear, yes, fear had a definite object; it was all right to worry about the fedayeen because the worry would depart when the threat passed. But among Stacey's random blows several struck a vital organ: my mode of enhancement and preservation, the subtle (because to the secret self our procedures are always subtle) way in which I worked the world while at the same time denying that I stood to gain. The anxiety came at the Dead Sea, the lowest spot on earth, entering through the arbitrary experience of a transient who has been blocked from reaching his usual evasions and hiding places. Becoming a lawyer, a certified winner, papered over the memory, but later I learned it could return before a judge (any judge), a case (any case), whether I was well-prepared or flying by the seat of my pants. Nothing is ever lost, least of all stabs of thought saying *me, me, me.*

My way out was to marry not only a woman, but the whole elaborate and extended network of her family. If upon taking this step we could have peered to the bottom of things, I'd have seen how much Connie needed to pull away from what I wanted to approach. With a new father, a second mother and the peerage of acquired siblings, I hoped to subdue my will; I longed for a given bias, traditions, claims I might honor. Not so farfetched a wish, though it soon fell victim to ill luck and the presumption that one could adopt a family without long years of apprenticeship. Three months after we trooped before the judge, a coronary seized Connie's father as he chased a tennis ball. Until the sharp turnaround brought on by her illness, Mary was at best an icicle, at worst my dueling partner. Connie's two brothers might as well live in Greenland. Her sister Lizzie is primarily concerned—justifiably, I might say—with her own needs. As for Connie herself, well, it soon became apparent that she was as much in search of a parent as I was, and that I had been nominated.

The Dead Sea was like the sun, impossible to hold in the eye. The air bounced off the desolate mountains of Moab and hung in a purple haze above the prism of the lake. It took three torturous hours to climb from the oasis at Ein Gedi to the Cave of the Martyrs, set deep in a canyon only a few miles away. There was no road from the sea or prospect of carrying dunnage up the cliffside, so the expedition approached across the plateau from the west, the trucks leaving us on a crag three hundred meters above the canyon floor. Here the Romans had come to starve out the Jews. One hundred soldiers pitched tents, posted lookouts, built a wall, cooked bread. The stones had fallen to the earth, but from a helicopter the outlines of the camp could be made out. With an aerial photograph held down by pebbles, the crew Connie and I were part of plotted where the rubble of boulders had stood in the year 134. No one had camped here since; no one had cared. We found a lamp nozzle and a coin, and felt blessed. Under the rocks were tarantulas.

We reached the cave by scampering down a path that led away from its mouth, until a hairpin turn forced us to hug the cliffside. Jumping from ledge to ledge, we reached a rope ladder swaying in gusts of air rolling in from the sea, climbing as they collided with the slope. Connie made her way like a gazelle, unconcerned by the height. To avoid looking down, I fixed my eyes onto the hips of this strange dancer.

We climbed through a slit into a vast chamber, built like a hive, then crawled through another passage to the deeper halls. Bats screamed as they flitted across the path of my torch, furious at the intrusion. In the play of lamp lights, stones fallen from the roof assumed menacing shapes. It was here, one hundred and fifty meters inside the mountain, at the innermost point, that the cave gave up its greatest secrets.

Bedouins had ransacked the place, grabbing what they could to sell to dealers in Amman and Jerusalem. But they had not come with pneumatic drills, photographers' lights, metal detectors or even army shovels. They took a few fragments of scroll, a sandal, a jug, and left stubbed-out Jordanian cigarettes in the sand near the entrance. The dryness that preserved everything made our faces brittle. We sifted every inch of rubble, piling earth in rubber baskets, dumping the debris into the wadi. From crevices formed where jagged ceiling met sandy floor we dug up goat shit, olive pits, sandal straps, oil lamps, a glass platter, mirrors, a net used to catch birds, a silver earring, vessels for cosmetics, arrowheads, bronze pitchers, and then human bones and skulls; finally, papyrus documents, and the letters of Shimeon Bar Kokhba, prince of all Israel. Whether Bar Kokhba, son of a star, or Bar Koziba, son of a deceiver, is not really known.

The papyri were legal documents and official correspondence. What remained after the centuries for us to read was the conveyance of property and calls for help. In the third year of Imperator Caesar Traianus Hadrianus Augustus, a farmer of the district of Zoar gave to his wife Miriam, the daughter of Joseph, the son of Manasseh, all that he possessed in Mahoza. In some detail the deed set out the boundaries and water rights. The farmer reserved the right to use the property as he wished until death, and the gift was conditional on Miriam's continued faithful service as his wife. The covenants were laid out in the jargon of the day, remarkably similar to our own. Among the papyri was a letter written in Hebrew by the embattled general to the men of nearby Ein Gedi. "Shalom: In comfort you sit, eat and drink from the property of the House of Israel, and care nothing for your brothers."

Here is the story, as it has come down to us. In A.D. 66 the Jews revolted against foreign domination. In their defeat Rome wasted the countryside, sacked Jerusalem and demolished the great temple. Later the fortress of Masada was captured after the Zealots put themselves to death rather than fall into Roman hands. As the Jews dispersed through the empire, sporadic rebellions were quelled by the Imperial army. But the last challenge to Rome before the Jews were totally scattered took place in Judea. In 132 Bar Kokhba, a brilliant general as all agree, succeeded in retaking Jerusalem and briefly reestablishing a Jewish state. Historians still dispute the causes of this last revolt. Some say the Jews simply could not abide foreign domination. Others find the source in the construction by the Romans of a shrine to Jupiter on the sacred site of the temple. According to a second-century biography of the Emperor, the Jews rebelled when Hadrian extended an earlier ban on castration to circumcision. At any rate, Bar Kokhba or Koziba, thought by some to be the Messiah, certainly an experienced soldier, dared to attack the Romans. For two years he startled the Empire by inflicting heavy losses on the legions, but eventually the Romans prevailed, destroying the main rebel force at a mountain retreat named Bethar, near Jerusalem. It is thought that Bar Kokhba's routed soldiers, his followers in Ein Gedi, fled before the troops of the Roman general Julius Severus, only to meet their fate in the cave. But we don't know if the last Jew thought to be the Messiah remained with them to the end. Yigael Yadin has concluded that the Romans on the cliff did not attack. Controlling the only source of water, torrents running down the wadi after a rain, they merely waited at their camp on the bluff. The men, women and children below could survive for just so long on the animals they had brought to the cave, water stolen at night, nesting birds. As punishment for the revolt, Hadrian issued a decree forbidding the Jews to lay eyes on Jerusalem. According to Yadin, references to Bar Kokhba in later Jewish sources are "ambivalent in nature: animosity towards a 'Messiah' who failed, combined with awe and admiration for a military hero."

I once worked for an idiotic, pot-bellied drunkard of a hotel owner named Morgenstern. He wore crimson trousers and yellow shirts as he teetered around the dining room discussing golf scores with his guests. His wife came in late to work on the books in the office. She was short to the staff, as if we were always getting in her way; she had hair the color of an apricot, and after all these years the memory of her rising chest can still arouse me. It was my job to pick her up every morning at eleven-thirty and take her to the hotel from the seaside ranch house where she and Morgenstern retired after the bar closed, like cats returning to their cage. When I arrived, she was still in her housecoat, sipping coffee from a mug, blowing smoke that hung above the plastic zebra-skin upholstery. I sat on a footrest and waited, staring at the ceiling or sneaking looks at her thighs. I oscillated between two fantasies, the conflict protecting me from mistake. In the first, I pushed up her silky cover and took her on the wall-to-wall carpet; in the second, at a signal she came to me, diving on the erection I was trying hard to conceal. Inside my head I batted the two around like a volleyball. It never occurred to me that neither would happen; it was just a question of picking the one I preferred. They both seemed right for an older woman who kept a bar, snapped at young people and awoke at eleven to sit around in a skimpy red bathrobe smoking in front of her driver. My pornography allowed her only these roles, but she never played them. For reasons beyond my youthful comprehension, she couldn't have cared less.

This month Connie's sister Lizzie is meditating in order to gather confidence and then express it in bio-energenics. "I am," she says, "your typical therapy junkie. I try everything, but nothing works." At other times she bangs a pillow with her tennis racket and screams, "I hate you, I hate you!"

Her guru frowns. "Now I want real hate. You're still on the surface."

Lizzie is less frantic when she stays away from the city, but she needs this succession of therapists because she cannot accept the worth of isolation. She says she wants to find herself in a novel and begs friends to put her in their books. The winter in upstate New York, where she lives, is so long and bleak that by February she settles for a TV series. "Put me in your sitcom," she pleads. "A small part will do. I could be the girl who calls a wrong number."

These days Lizzie is trying to come to terms with the ego deflation brought on by her Ohmygod syndrome: the sudden arrival of the dreadful conviction that she's fucked up again. We're flying to California to play tennis: "Ohmygod, I forgot my tennis shoes. Where are my sun glasses? Ohmygod, I left them on the bureau." Total anxiety and threat focused on a loss or mistake that usually hasn't happened.

"The glasses are in your purse," Connie tells her sister. "Ohmygod."

"We are a nation of kisses," writes my secret admirer, "so it should be nothing special, but your greeting kiss stirred thoughts of a whole new life. The fantasy excites me. I crave. You move me. You open a door. I want no complications, no seriousness, merely to desire openly. But making the first move is awkward. How do men learn how to do it? But I must have courage. When your mustache brushed against my lips, I wanted to feel you deep in my mouth. I pray you won't ignore me or pretend you don't know that I am the one who wrote this letter."

It is unsigned, and I have no idea who wrote it. My frustration must be fit punishment for lechery, the price of too often casually speaking a sexual language. She mentions a dream we've discussed. A dream and a kiss. Days of preoccupation arc spent in trying to place them.

The letter stuns me. Which of my many estimable qualities produces such adoration? Or is this merely a tease? I must know. I become John Le Carré—or rather George Smiley—but without the research facilities of Whitehall or a crime lab I must rely on my wits. It is the very task I need; brushed aside are manuscripts, briefs and bills; thoughts about judgeships, human rights and administration. Conceptualization, the process of having ideas, is where I think I am best. When his cases get too frustrating, Rudy talks about the need for a business called Ideas, Inc. I differ with him only about the consumer potential. He thinks the world is anxious to buy new ideas; I am dubious. Most of the time, if you want to know where people will be tomorrow, look at yesterday.

"It may be," Rudy says, "that the architecture of the brain and the structure of language express a preference for routinized thinking and so favor the past." He speculates that incentives are necessary to overcome this tendency—a possible justification for capitalism.

In any event, I work at conceptualization; through fantasy, I play the Sherlock Holmes of free association. But first, like a good detective, I catalog the facts. An unmarked envelope typed on a frayed ribbon with the wrong address, so written by someone who doesn't work in the building—unless, of course, this is a cunning device to throw me off the track, but there's no motive for that. Her expectation is instant recognition. How could I fail to recognize such purity, such ardor, not to mention good judgment? I am supposed to know who wants my body, who I have greeted with a kiss, who has told me a dream. I make a long list. It will be an insult if I don't divine. With few exceptions the text is about her erotica and its consequences, the joy of expressing an inhibition overcome, the joy of letting it all hang out, the joy of the future. But I simply don't remember lingering looks as my mustache tickled a face. Despite the enthusiasm, the letter is too well written for a put-on. Besides, do I have an enemy who writes that well? I imagine myself with every woman on the list. The postmark is the nineteenth. Grabbing my appointment book, I read the story of my life for the last two months. A few leads, but no likely ones. I decide that facts don't help; they are only the proscenium for fantasy. After weeks of discreet allusions to potential candidates and aimless searching for clues, dipping again into my diary and shuffling my phone book, I am lost and not getting found. Whether this is revenge or fear on her part I'm not sure, but eventually even an obsession turns tedious. I decide to give myself two more weeks of sneaking looks at the letter before tearing it up.

But I still have it. When I want to comfort myself, I dig the letter out from the depths of a bottom drawer to study the promise and past fused by our arrangements, even this one.

Work

I WENT into this line of work not to run a courtroom or a law school, but to drive the South with people like Harold Duff. Despite the heat of the day, between Americus and Albany we slow down to ten miles an hour to avoid the wrath of High Sheriff Sarker, who once bloodied Duff with an ax handle. Sarker repays our prudence with moderation and merely tickets the vehicle for a dirty license plate and dusty bumpers. At five feet ten and two hundred pounds, Sarker must be the dwarf of Georgia sheriffs. He saunters around the car as if he's thinking of buying it, then pokes his watermelon-size head into the back seat, obviously hoping we're hauling bales of marijuana.

"You heah, Harold, the Federals gonna use the A-tomic bomb on us. Sweep the county clean."

"Now, Sheriff, they wouldn't do that to the pecan crop."

"Ah don't know."

Bubbling over with constitutional rights, I want to object to this violation of the First, Fourth, Fifth and Fourteenth amendments, but I hesitate, pondering the consequences. Sarker might force me to commit an unnatural act. The FBI agents, half a mile back at a filling station pretending they're having trouble with a Coke machine, would take notes and later dictate a lengthy report. As all communications from special agents are addressed to the director, J. Edgar himself might read of my injuries. But neither Sarker nor Duff would pay any attention if I complained. The steps in their gavotte have been handed down over the generations; indifferent to laws and Northerners, they deal without intermediaries.

"Hear they made a fuss over by Blaisdell's."

"Just your ordinary case of riotous and insurrectionary conduct, Sheriff."

"That county's outta mah jurisdiction."

Duff takes the hint. "Wouldn't consider a protest *here*."

"Goo-d."

"Be on our way."

"You take care now, Harold. Don't let no one burn your house down."

"Be a blessing. I doubled the insurance. Would make me a rich man. Bye now."

The disguise that is Duff's face brings to mind a Northern reporter who bought us drinks to celebrate the end of Jim Crow in New Orleans restaurants before going off to stuff himself with gumbo. He bought a gas mask in preparation for the arrival of the first black on the campus of the University of Mississippi. Hidden behind the plastic snout, he roamed the campus at will, enjoying the smoke bombs and flares of his first riot, taking no more than a whiskey bottle on the head as he scribbled madly in his notebook. Then he saw the dead Frenchman lying by his camera, eight thousand miles from home to cover the story. The marshals had left him stretched out on the close-cropped campus grass until a wagon came to pick up the body. It was the first dead man the reporter had seen; milling about with his colleagues, most of them masked, he began to weep, dropping huge, wet tears down the funnel. He could not rip the thing off and cry openly. Later he included in his expense account an item for $29.25: "one gas mask." Three months after the smog cleared from Oxford, the paper returned his requisition with a curt memo ordering him to put down the purchase as lunch.

When Teddy is arrested for making a phone call from the white waiting room of the Jackson train station, our boss in New York sends a wire reprimanding him. He's forgotten that as a lawyer his place is in court, not in the trenches. Teddy is advised to please get himself on the critical list next time he contemplates direct action, or at least be soundly thrashed so Good Works can raise funds on his battered black body.

After the assassinations the money rolls in, but following the riots the mailbags are full of angry letters from contributors charging that we've turned into subversives. On the WATS line the throat-clearing has that authoritative G-man sound; occasionally I hear the regular clicking of a tape switching spools. Connie announces she has sat through her last rendition of *We Shall Overcome* at about the time I start getting postage-due packages with dead mice. My favorite token of affection is the hangman's noose, tied by a professional. I—we—have done nothing different. I—we—write our endless briefs, take our three-day depositions, try cases when we have to and fly little planes across the bayous.

One sultry morning after breakfast Duff and I snake two hundred miles up the turnpike to state prison to see Billy Lee Lemon on Death Row. A local boy, Lemon's case had been kicking around the courts for years. Duff was his trial lawyer. Good Works took over for the appeals. Neither of us remembers much about the crime except that Lemon was the wheelman. After an all-night crap game, he and a friend held up a grocery store, netting forty-two dollars. The friend gunned down the storekeeper, but he confessed first and was given five years in exchange for testifying against Billy Lee. The friend is now on the street. We keep Lemon alive by challenging every comma in the state's capital-punishment law, but let the case linger once it becomes apparent that the trial judge now thinks it's in the court of appeals and the court of appeals thinks it's back with the lower court. Not appearing on anybody's docket, no execution date has been set; Billy Lee has fallen between the cracks. The last thing we want is to remind anyone that he exists, but now with the help of a jailhouse lawyer he has fired of a petition to the federal courts asserting his constitutional right to a color television set.

While Duff goes in to persuade the warden to let Lemon have the tube, I browse in the gift shop. Inmates have taken agates and tiger's eyes and carefully set them in polished silver. They lie on pool-table felt in an old wooden display case. Under each piece is the convict's name on a white card: BRACELETS BY MAD DOG BURKE. RINGS BY RONNIE THE RAPIST.

As usual, I can tell nothing from Duff's face. "The warden says there's a regulation prohibiting the condemned from mingling with the rest of the prison population. The TV room is in Block B; Lemon is in Block A. He can't move from A to B because that's the rules. You know, that bracelet wasn't made by Mad Dog Burke. He franchises his name for ten percent of the take. The merchandise moves faster when the customer thinks it was made by a ghoul."

We visit Lemon, hoping to persuade him to withdraw the suit before the state attorney general's office figures out there's no death date in his file. The guards make us empty our pockets before letting us through the metal detector; they even keep our belts. Waiting for Lemon in the visitors' room, I begin to feel the absence of change, wallet and keys. To fill the emptiness I reach for my cigarettes, but they too have been confiscated. It takes me five minutes with Lemon before I work up the nerve to bum a smoke. He is adamant about the lawsuit. "It ain't fair," he says. "I don't mind not being able to work or eat in the mess hall or play ball in the yard with the rest, but they gotta give me somethin'." When Duff explains that the case may alert the courts to their oversight, Lemon goes blank; it is plain that he too has forgotten. Seven years after the crime he no longer recalls the crap game, the moonshine, the wheel, the white man bleeding to death in the doorway of his Seven-Eleven market.

Seven years is a long time to remember anything clearly, even when you've been sentenced to death for it, but in my experience criminals— and the guilty part the rest of us law-abiding types are willing to admit to—demonstrate a remarkable incidence of amnesia. One might think this came from confusing the crime with the inevitable exculpatory story, except that to call the tales they come up with lame would be an act of kindness. Their alibis are simply too crippled in imagination, though often rendered with great conviction, to cause the storyteller to forget what actually happened. I believe memory fails criminals because they don't believe the crimes were theirs in the first place. They think these transgressions—and the vast majority know the difference between what is legal and illegal—belong to the powerful others who they feel ordered their commission. These others include people as well as circumstance. Even flags are sometimes to blame. These others, not the offenders, own the criminal acts as a result of directing that they must occur.

I sensed nothing of this at the time and was crushed by our interview with Lemon. Here was a man trifling with the gas chamber because he'd been deprived of a box that emitted prattle and pretty colors. He'd rather die than do without pictures of a life he could never have, and had never led in the first place. As caretaker of this dummy's slim chances to die of natural causes I had, of course, been thwarted, but this wasn't important. No, lawyers and clients regularly screw up each other's plans—so much so that a social scientist would label such behavior as the norm. Rather, it was that Lemon reminded me how gorplike nourishing, how necessary, seems power, even the ersatz power of the tube, to those who are powerless. I like to think the child in me, not the adult, requires such infusions, but actually there is no such neat division. It is the powerless part that needs colors in a box to believe that the self will survive.

Until the war ended and Nixon's hash was settled, each morning began without doubt, the agenda prepared in advance. Suddenly our lives have turned inward. We watch the divorces of our friends, get to know our children, probate a parent's will, review books, buy a house in the country. I return to old things, beginnings, the way a diver visits the blue tang, the sergeant major, the squirrel fish still hovering by the crevices of a favorite reef. In Clare's family no one speaks to everyone. She talks to her father, her father to her mother, her mother to one son, the other son only to Maharaj Ji. Clare now threatens to give up the law and become a family therapist. Lizzie, a third born of four, doesn't think she belongs. Rudy, the fiercest competitor of them all, has an older brother. An only child, everything I do or feel is unique. Naturally. My cousin Philo treats the game of families as science, charting the sixty-four basic conflicts between parent and child, but I employ the game to cover the skittish first moments of a difficult social encounter. Find out the age and sex of siblings—of parents, spouse, children if there is time—and I have a way of talking to people about something that matters. According to Walter Toman's classic treatment of the subject, new relationships tend to duplicate the earliest; the closer the fit between new and old, the better off we are. Imagine picking a jury on family rank. The system isn't foolproof, but I prefer it to astrology.

My pictures of the sixties have always been difficult to develop. The competence and legal skill of Annie, Rudy and me were indispensable but unwanted. The biggest sixties word was *system*. The system was bad but you had to deal with it, even if just to piss in its face. And we were around to do the dealing, shuttling back and forth between the dreamers and politicians, unloved by both camps. The radicals loathed our loyalty to vocation because having rules means that everything is not possible; the pols detested us because neutral principles are their greatest enemy. A fixed role, a daily slogging up the hill and down, a set of skills, the elitism that follows from possessing them—all these are alien to the state of mind and spirit that is our legacy from the decade. Of course, we certainly never thought out the position we took. Where we ended up had less to do with intellectual analysis than with the fact that as children we weren't allowed to make a mess. The present generation may be politically illiterate, but at least it knows in its bones that childhood has to be lived out to be forgotten.

Alone in the middle of the Antarctic waste, Admiral Byrd believes he is dying of carbon monoxide fumes. His spirit wanes until he remembers the fear of losing as he wrestled for the welterweight championship of the Naval Academy. Not wanting to bring shame to his mother in the gallery, he determined to triumph. He grows enfeebled, but he is one hundred twenty-three miles from his main base at Little America. Refusing to alarm men who would lose their lives to save him, he dissembles on the radio. Each morning when he awakes, the temperature in his plywood and aluminum hut hovers near minus forty degrees. A stove, his only defense against freezing, is the source of the gas. Choosing the lesser evil, he poisons himself to keep warm, and writes letters begging forgiveness from his family.

The world has been told that Byrd is at an advance base to conduct meteorological research, but he knows he is there as a test of will and to learn to live more deeply within himself. "Real peace comes from struggle that involves such things as effort, discipline, enthusiasm. This is also the way to strength. An inactive peace may lead to sensuality and flabbiness, which are discordant. It is often necessary to fight to lessen discord. This is the paradox." Playing Beethoven's Fifth on a crank-handle record player, the Admiral mounts a ladder to the observation hatch, where he is overcome by an electronic madness of rippling lights from the southern aurora. In the delusion brought on by illness, the music and the sky are one. After three and a half months his men come for him, but he has never asked for help. He thinks of himself as a middleman between theory and fact.

The crowd behaved strangely. Hmms and rasps peaked and bottomed out, came and went, as if someone were making rapid twists of the volume control on a stereo. The screams hushed a fraction of a second too soon, followed by a self-conscious murmur. A firm sense of this being just another day meant that it wasn't. We were being watched. Ebbets Field was not demonstrating an absence of bigotry—far from it—but expropriating Robinson as its own. It was easy to read the entrails. He was 0 for 3, but late in the game dropped so perfect a bunt down the first-base line that the usually slick-fielding Earl Torgeson sailed the ball into right field. Robby breezed into second, Stanky went to third, and both scored when Pete Reiser doubled down the line.

A few days later the Phillies caught him between third and home. He danced that wicked catch-me-if-you-can dance, faked toward the plate, hesitated, dashed back to third base and then again to home, where he was tagged out. But the batter had made it to third on a ground ball to the infield. Robby was fast, but it wasn't the speed. Here was a man running for his life: The Little Engine That Could.

In the prepared text of my statement to the legislative committee looking into an epidemic of mugging, I claim that we can't get rid of the one hundred fifty million guns in this country because every man has to feel the business world remains open to him. "Those of my clients who pass through the criminal courts are the most energetic, ambitious and upwardly mobile in the ghetto. They feel this is the only form of entrepreneurial expression left open to them."

In response to these heresies the Republican-Conservative legislator from upstate professes shock. His body movement questions my manhood, his intonation my motives, but his words merely ask for my authority. If I'd been talking to Rudy, I would have quoted Veblen: "The ideal pecuniary man is like the ideal delinquent in his unscrupulous conversion of goods and persons to his own ends, and in a callous disregard of the feelings and wishes of others and of the remoter effects of his actions, but he is unlike him in possessing a keener sense of status and in working more far-sightedly to a remoter end." With Binni I might have said, "Look, this is my experience, it needn't be yours," but to the right honorable member from Oneonta I can only cite a court of law. "It was said by a judge in *Feeble v. Syzmanski*." I carry these names around in my head, and there is no luggage room where they can be abandoned. *Mapp, Molloy, Palsgraf*, and *Martin v. Hunter's Lessee* and *Fletcher v. Peck*: each stands for a rule, a set of facts, a prophecy. Thus I play the law game, with its carving of the self into little segments. I tell my students their role will be ever-changing. They must learn to ask: Where am I? Who else is there? What do I and they want? What happens next, and what came before?

Connie and I try to list the people we know who think they work in order to earn a living. None of our friends are on it. In a variation on this theme Rudy reminds me that both of us have always been employees of nonprofit organizations. We have been institutionalized. When the San Francisco Mime Troupe did Goldoni on Wooster Street during the sixties, three actors stepped across the footlights into the audience. With swords drawn, devilishly fingering the blades, they demanded that the foundation scout reveal himself. In my party the salaries of all the males and two-thirds of the females were traceable to tax-exempt contributions. The one exception was a shrink.

No blacks lived near my childhood house on the Island. Except for straw-hatted old men bottom-fishing from the causeway in the oily waters of the bay, they were rarely found on the flatlands. The few I recall clustered in the lee of the Irish gangs that roamed Funland, the penny arcades and the boardwalk, looking for victims. I shared with the blacks only the tactic of looking insignificant.

Then there was General Oglethorpe. One day my father announced that we were going away. He didn't so much tell me as advertise the trip. "In the winter, no less. A swimming pool, tennis courts and three huge meals a day. And we're going by Pullman, so you can eat breakfast in a dining car. The General Oglethorpe Hotel in Savannah, Georgia." Then, slipping into his Mel Allen voice, "How 'bout that!" He flashed a glossy brochure showing a tall, balding black in a white coat welcoming a bright-eyed smiling couple under the oak-shaded pillars of a huge mansion.

I knew something about the Georgia prison colony, but none of the toothy people in the brochure lounging pool-side, sipping long drinks from frosted glasses, looked like criminals, or even like Mr. Hurley, the neighbor who snarled when I crossed his lawn and climbed on his porch to retrieve a ball from under the wicker chairs. Not having a gun for this voyage of discovery, I packed my machete, bought on Delancey Street from a peddler who insisted it had been used to hack Japs to death on Okinawa.

Connie is incredulous when I tell her that as a child I carried a six-inch

blade to protect myself at a gentile resort hotel, but then her main ethnic identification is the weekly purchase of lean Nova Scotia—from a little
place we know where they slice the salmon like jewelers cutting diamonds.
Not that I'm so different. My Judaism emerges from the threat of defeat.
As a twelve-year-old, it was brought on by the Irish gangs—that is, by bel-
ligerent non-Jews. My attachment to the Israelis grows if they look like
losers. A few Nazis march in Illinois and I stand on the First Amendment.
Twenty years ago, when the preppy dean interviewing me for admission
to Harvard signaled modified rapture by taking calls and shuffling papers,
I read it not as anti-Semitism, but as the arrogance of the elite. Even then
they admitted enough New Yorkers from public schools with signs of so-
cialism and salesman fathers, even with shit-eating grins like mine. I didn't
blame the dean for the fact that the competition was tight if you weren't
from Hotchkiss; the worst thing about the meritocracy was that I wasn't
in it. Vanity allowed no other explanation. Still, I know no easier object of
contempt than a man who has changed his name. Thoughts of moving out
of the city induce hay fever. Rudy counts it a good week when he hasn't
dreamed of Hitler.

Out of reach in the back closet is an ancient photograph of the young
master embarking on this journey. A corduroy jacket, gray slacks, an open
shirt worn over the collar and a hat, a junior-size version of the wide-brim
from Knox the Hatter that my father wore to cover his bald head—his salesman hat. The extraordinary thing about this picture is the buck-toothed,
crew-cut, apprehensive face peering out from behind a wall of glass. The
world could not have been a friendly place. How could any good come of
such a visage? My children have their problems, but nothing like that. No
welfare mother of my acquaintance has children who look so miserable.

The colored cars put me onto it. Somewhere around Washington, after
we pushed our noses against the glass to catch a glimpse of the Capitol,
there was some rearranging. The next time I snaked back through the swaying train to the rear observation car, the faces were all black. Never having
seen so many before in one place, I felt transported to Africa, some Tarzan
movie of the mind. Years later, watching a four-block queue weave through
the streets of Johannesburg to the Soweto bus depot, I was able to piece
together the young traveler and the Seaboard Railroad. This was humanity
unadorned, stripped of pretense, hunkering down for survival. The sight
lay on the stomach like dumpling soup for later digestion. In Savannah the
sun was shining. As we hustled our bags down the long platform to the
street, I asked my mother about COLORED WAITING ROOM and WHITE
WAITING ROOM in the voice a child uses to get attention from preoccu-

pied adults. A man in a gray striped suit, vested, a watch chain crawling across his belly, turned and stared, lips curling. The age-old disapproval of an elder, remembered long after loss of virginity, wedding day and Supreme Court arguments. Withering, reproachful, disgusted, casting me out.

The summer residents of this island are rich enough to scorn talk of money, intelligent enough to divine their plight, humane enough to pause before they act. They are placed so that hustling is an embarrassment. Each summer house dotting the dunes is stuffed with good things: freshly dug clams, wheels of Brie, young children running in packs. They are healthy, have a quota for eggs, drink white wine on cedar decks that command the sea; they play tennis daily, sail, take long walks on the beach. Every Sunday on the island I take my children to the softball game. The men I watch approach the mystery of play, of purposive movement.

The players come with borrowed gloves, balls gray and scuffed, bats held like clubs. Nine-year-olds watch the daddies. In July the first game starts at ten, but as the summer grows so does the urgency. By August they begin by nine-thirty. Latecomers must wait.

There are insiders and outsiders. The insiders always choose the players, and choose themselves unless one of the newer summer people has a special look: jeans hitched at a no-nonsense angle, a confident warmup drift under a towering fly ball. As the teams are chosen, the men paw the ground with their sneakers and to avoid looking at the captains stare out at the shingle roof in deep center field near the state road. The players are culled from the cluster near the mound, leaving a pool of losers to sit out the first game, waiting impatiently and ignominiously for the second.

The losers shuffle off to toss a ball with the children, or offer to umpire. The pitchers are always the same. The psychiatrist from New Jersey has come here beyond the longest memory. Does he dream of the strike zone all winter long as his patients rant, is real life here and all the rest hot-stove league? The game itself is full of stops and starts. Men loll around the bases and contemplate the eelgrass while the catcher chases dogs off the diamond. The "Atta baby, atta baby" of the third baseman could be a Hail Mary. When the ball is pitched, I feel the total concentration of the senses that marks a moment of ecstasy. Of course, there are some who don't really care: weekend visitors brought along for the treat, a landmark visited like the cliffs; men so awkward they can't even imagine over-the-shoulder stabs running away from the plate in rabbit-holed left field. To the college kids who are still close to a physical existence, this is only another game, but for the rest of us a moment has arrived. We still daydream of Bobby Thomson.

It disappointed my father that I never could sell anything, but there was a brazenness in the family heritage that I could swallow and turn to use. For giving cigarettes away, fifty dollars a months wasn't bad. Jed saw it as a sign that I was learning. The Teamsters broke the quiet of the street behind Burton Hall as they hauled the boxes to the door of the gray frame house. Like a parade of natives on safari, my housemates carried the cartons of giveaway five-packs upstairs and stacked them in my room. They drooled for a tip and departed, pockets bulging. I became a walking carcinogen, giving away smokes in dining halls, the snack bar, in front of the library. "Try a Marlboro." I had no trouble, made instant friends, could have run for office. I felt bad about submitting phony reports, but I couldn't bring myself to ask my peers whether they preferred hard pack to soft. "Describe the reaction to the new hard pack," commanded the report form. "Pardon me, I am taking a survey. Could you tell me your response to the hard pack? What about the tattoo on the Marlboro man? Does the smoke tickle your nose on its way to the throat?"

There must have been an executive in New York who monitored these reports, and seeing mine, grabbed for the hot line. "Hurry, get me marketing. Hello, chief, the new hard pack is making headway against Winston in the heartland. We're crushing the opposition on the campuses of America." It was my first feeble contribution to fucking up capitalism. It had taken guts to get the job. I'd walked in cold and talked my way past a receptionist to see Mr. Dodds, the chief of college marketing, a dead ringer for the young Dana Andrews. Dodds puffed incessantly, as if the company handed out demerits to workers caught not smoking on the job. He seemed sincerely concerned that my school had pushers for Liggett & Myers, American Tobacco and Reynolds, but none for Philip Morris. Considering its academic distinction, a shocking omission. Tutored by my father, I left it at that; Dodds would have to check it out with whoever clutched the greasy pole above him, Jed predicted. "Tell him to consider the possibility; leave your name, and go quickly." A month later the boxes arrived. My Methodist landlady was disturbed, but she was a confirmed Viceroy addict.

Rushing to the front of the room before the arrival of the professor we called Young Black Bob, my classmate Donal mimics him beautifully with an artist's rendering of a defense against a prosecution for cannibalism.

There is always, *always* an argument, reads Young Black Bob's credo. "From time out of mind," Donal proclaims, "the courts have protected the right to eat what we please. If a man's home is his castle, what can we say of his plate? Take the precedent of the Donner party. In a criminal case such as the one we have at bar, the statute must be construed strictly, giving the accused every benefit. Unless the court can find beyond peradventure of a doubt that the legislature contemplated a prohibition on the mastication of human flesh, the conduct alleged in the indictment must be excluded from the ambit of the rule. Not a scintilla of evidence has been introduced to suggest that the coequal branch sought to regulate the culinary tastes of the citizenry."

Young Black Bob was an original. We were pleased to know him in his Freudian phase. Disdaining the showy viciousness of some of his colleagues, he cultivated silence, his only role to ask the first question and adopt a skeptical scowl. After gaining his perch before the class, he issued the day's provocation: "Why is rape a crime?" We went for the chum like hungry tuna. Mooting first principles, we must have believed he knew exactly what he was doing, while we were fools. He shot us down with his silence, but we never complained. Appearances must be kept. In certain settings it is acceptable, even encouraged, to tell friends, acquaintances, associates, colleagues or co-workers that they're not in touch with their feelings, that they're blocking, confused, angry, mistaken, exaggerating or insensitive to the rights of others. But in law school it is beyond the pale, taboo, strictly *verboten* to tell other people they're dumb. Such insults are rare because stupidity is on everyone's mind, a sin never forgiven or forgotten. After fifty minutes of watching us squirm, Young Black Bob would deliver thirty seconds of professing. "So one might say.... " he'd begin as the fish swarmed over chunks of squid. At the bell he disappeared to the Gothic gloom of his private office. Today we would call him a facilitator.

Young Black Bob embraced his stereotype, the Platonic image of himself, in so tight a hammerlock that he would be remembered-far longer than the others, but the soul of law school did not dwell at the extremes. The Socratic method, after all, is someone else's rigged deck, fearsome only to the Thracymachus in us, the toady. The real message of *The Way*, as I like to call it, acted as did the varnish so often applied to the ancient desks, the long library tables stacked high with books each thicker than a loaf of pumpernickel, that it had become indistinguishable from the grain. *The Way* was not mentioned, though a guiding principle of our work was that we were there to examine everything. I think of Sam, who measures his impact—a big word for him now that he is settled in Washington—by slavishly applying the simple rule that what his adversary does not mention is what concerns both of them most.

So it was at law school. We had come to have while others had not, to lead while they followed, to control while they scattered—as well as to learn to keep a left raised against unpredictable jabs from the great, unwieldy, expanding and contracting glop beyond our grassy cloister. No matter how many rationalizations were offered, for a guilt never acknowledged, assimiliation to the ways of having, leading and controlling had its disturbing side—especially since at the end of three years we were supposed to feel honored. With typical vigor, Young Black Bob and his colleagues offered the creative solution of splitting up. They taught the law but between classes tried to change it. They preached neutrality but with conviction. Schizophrenia, Philo tells me, is sometimes the best solution available to his patients. So we, their children, mimicked the routines of our mentors. Three for me and one for them. Keep your head down and learn the craft so that one day you'll be ready for the despotism to turn beneficent. A hard afternoon in the board room but dinner with that committee at the bar association.

Years later I spent many hours distracting myself from the anxieties of flying southward in various Lockheed Electras—planes lately modified to keep their wings from falling off—by attempting to understand my escape from this garden. I assumed that I'd escaped rather than made a choice. The redeeming social value of my work, the lower salary, the greater prestige of sacrifice, satisfied me only in the splendid but momentary warmth of a pretty woman's respect. Most of the time I could claim no virtue for it. I had not chosen, but for reasons unknown I contained too much anger, was too much an only child, to belong in a majority. Certainly I was as attracted to *having* as the rest of my class; it was just that I'd been driven elsewhere by gusts of biography.

In any event, I bought peace among ego, superego and id by a complex sleight of hand, a refinement worthy of a Wittgenstein, a Talmudist—well, a lawyer. The brownie points had to be scratched, but I could secretly exult at my own experience, keeping a scrapbook while my peers sat nailed to corporate bylaws. It was only later that Manny teased me into recognizing my worth. He tipped me to the importance of *and*. Events had yielded my tendency toward good works, *and* I had chosen. Both could be true at the same time. But you know how difficult to accept, how self-serving as we say around the courthouse, is this sort of shaky hindsight.

Donal was one of those very few who knew exactly why he was at law school. He boasted of a fabulous series of summer jobs close to the scent of influence—a runner on Wall Street, mail room at CBS, researcher at *Time* and junior associate grip at Universal. Go right to the source, he recommended. Donal would do a year with a judge in the District of Columbia, the kind who relishes trying seven-year-old antitrust cases between the Justice Department and DuPont; then a short stretch with a firm, a connection on the Hill, legislative assistant to an up-and-coming border-state senator, and then out by himself, a lawyer's lawyer, a fixer's fixer.

When they posted interview sign-up sheets, I realized that for openers bright young things were being offered salaries it took my father fifteen years of pavement pounding to earn. Even taking inflation into account, I plainly had to self-destruct. At my interview with a ruddy-faced, over-weight partner at Covert & Boring, I made the mistake of asking how late in the day associates were expected to stick around the office. Opening my fly would have produced no greater effect. Then I innocently inquired whether there would be an opportunity at this eminent firm to work on criminal cases. "My dear young man," replied the scandalized partner, with the solemnity that I associate with bullshit, "we like to think our men have excelled first in their own specialty—tax, real property or securities, as the case may be—before we entrust them with the liberty of a felon." His white hair seemed painted on with an airbrush. Why would anyone who had written a paper comparing Hobbes and Rousseau, I wondered, spend his few potent years laboring on something called securities? After taking the bar, I left the country.

Now they all want to go to law school. Between the ages of twenty-five and thirty-five, mostly female. The phone rings once a month for encouragement. Attention must be paid to lawyers, they say; do, don't talk; not at the mercy of bosses. A lawyer, they tell me in dead earnest, is definite, not just part of an organization but occupant of a special place. Public appearance. A weapon, though whether offensive or defensive, strategic or tactical, psychological or economic, is not clear. They never talk about the clients. And how could they at this point understand, much less arm themselves against, the corruption that goes along with being in the pay of those you dominate? The more benign, socially conscious candidates probably believe they'll make friends of their clients, as if friendship were possible between principal and agent. As this is also my operational illusion, any doubts I might raise would be feeble. At this point all they really want is *in;* they hear selectively.

Still, someone has to tell them that indoctrination leaves permanent scars, so I ask gently if they're willing to live without poetry, for example to see *The Merchant of Venice* not as a play but as a case—a case of a fool for a client at that. Read Antonio's contract with Shylock. The terms don't say anything about a jot of blood, but if a pound of flesh was owed, the law will imply what is necessary to get it. Or as a Somali once told the Baroness

Blixen, Shylock could have scraped off little bits at a time until he got his pound. If that doesn't satisfy you, I can cite a dozen cases standing for the rule that a claimant can take less than is due.

This week's call for encouragement comes from a woman who makes a list of jobs that she hopes will "validate" her. She picks apart her options in fine lawyerly fashion. Will she get to court? Will she get stuck in trusts and estates? Will she play cog to big wheels? All her concerns are quite sensible, but I wish she'd decide her future without involving me. I have enough problems of my own, and she's only called because she really wants to be me or what she supposes me to be. Nothing personal, mind you, she wants the role—the assemblage of clues, signs, fronts that are taken for something to respect. I tell her I've lost my taste for practice; she should treat me like an old fart, a sourpuss. She simply doesn't hear. "All right," I say, "which sort of work you choose matters less than you think. As far as I can tell, there isn't much difference between Lambchop, Hambone or the U.S. Attorney or Sly & Crafty because work alone doesn't validate; there must be something else." It is an unsatisfactory consultation. I am losing my touch as counselor.

I still don't remember the dream and greeting kiss referred to by my secret admirer. Though who can remember dreams and kisses? They grow on trees.

The crowd at the premier of *The Battle of Algiers* is dressed to kill. There are cheers for every dead *pied noir*. I can barely breathe for the burning grass. As we leave for dinner, a friend sums it up: "It all depends on whose ox is gored." We go to an Italian restaurant near Canal Street owned by one of his union clients. On the Chianti label are the Towers of San Gimignano. Naïvely, I take the seat facing the door. The client asks me to switch chairs with him. "Is this for real," I ask my friend, "or does he do it to amuse the tourists?"

"In a bargaining session they occasionally signal us to fold for less than the going rate. We get the message. It's a family matter."

As I wait at Foley Square for Bernie, my student assistant, to arrive with our papers, I'm thinking that every city-side reporter who can ride the subway has done night court, the juvenile lockups, Rikers Island and Family Court, but the story of Special Term has yet to be written. It's too much a lawyer's joke. A calendar call of one hundred fifty cases a day, messengers yelling "submitted," "ready for," "application," motions thrown at the clerks, stuffed in brown envelopes and marched off in little piles to be decided by an army of law secretaries. Occasionally a judge gets interested and actually wields the stamp of justice himself. These days it is plastic, not rubber.

Our client hasn't a leg to stand on. The city is about to evict her from public housing into a nursing home. The social workers are against her because she believes in spirits. In her more senile moments she menaces old ladies in the elevator, plays her dead husband's Gene Krupa records at full volume and screams obscenities in the mail room. In short, just a normal New Yorker. All would be forgiven if she had wit enough to let the social workers talk her out of the evil eye and provide the services they were trained to deliver. She belongs in Haiti, but no one is left there to take her in. Her son doesn't return our calls. The city wants her apartment. She mutters curses at both son and system over a farina-smelling cauldron on her stove. Her kitchen is purple. My fantasy is that she was once the madam of a fancy whorehouse.

Our strategy is delay. With a few breaks we hope to hold the sheriff off for two years, by which time our client will be dead or the case so stale that we can bargain. We have judge-shopped and landed a well-known jurist who is under investigation for selling appointments. His son-in-law has more wards than Bellevue. This month we hope to discover an untypical sensitivity to the downtrodden. Before the regular audience of runners, barrators and bored associates from elegant Wall Street firms, we hope he will take advantage of us to display what a good fellow he really is. In this court you must plead on the run because the clerk calls the next case before you reach the bar. Shouting to muffle the din, we make our pitch. What we're not prepared for is the little speech. "Outstanding papers. Highest responsibility of the bar. *Pro bono publico*. I will grant your motion because you are involved in public service, but next time, please, *please* be ready to proceed."

"Please!" Bernie exclaims, lurching toward the door before the judge changes his mind. "The grand jury must be hot on his trail."

As the city teeters on the edge of bankruptcy like a drunk on a bridge, Arabs pay fancy prices in soggy petrodollars for a piece of our unlivable rock. One school believes they are hypnotized by pop. New Yorkers cannot credit rumors that oil princes have been lured here by the promise of stability or a preference for individual to clan violence. Never having seen an Arab on the IRT or read Doughty, we are skeptical of news that they will soon own Morgan Guaranty. My own theory is that Arabs are as layered as Jews. The more urbane pump their assets to Geneva or London, but there are some who, even in fabulous retirement, must keep the past in sight— like old sea captains who nail a wheel to the parlor floor and spend hours staring at the sea. They have come because the shifting sands, the arbitrariness of our fortunes, remind them of what their life used to be. Lizzie is afraid they'll make a tender for Zabar's in order to secretly double the nitrates in Genoa salami.

What scenes await them. The Israeli handyman offers me a battery, but his booster has been stolen. O'Rourke will lend me the cables after he cleans the steps of his brownstone; I take the shovel from his hand and finish the job while he disappears into the cellar. On the street the three of us huddle under the hood of my beached whale. The old man clamps the claws to the terminal, but the engine refuses to turn.

"Rusty jumpers," says the Israeli. My guess is that he has been here less than five years.

"This battery is too weak," O'Rourke replies, his voice gravelly. He was born somewhere in Queens, though his father was from the Old Country.

"Da greeps are...lookit." The Israeli scrapes a few puny sparks with the claws.

"Whatdjatalkinabout. No juice."

"Leeson, Imalectrician."

O'Rourke turns to me. "He's an electrician. I'm a master electrician. Forty years. A union man." He can barely contain himself.

Again the Israeli mutters, "Rusty jumpers."

I fear O'Rourke is about to hit him when the Chinaman with the toy poodle comes along. They wave him to the car.

"Whadjatink of dis?"

"Saw lights on last night," clippedy-clop. "Didn't know it yours," clippedy-clop. Postwar. He arrived as a young man in the late forties when Mao mopped up the Nationalists.

"Would've told. Would've told."

"Dead battery."

"Sheetee cables."

Under the hood they shout, gesture, grimace. I step back. This no longer concerns me; I am merely the patient. In anger O'Rourke folds up his jumpers, the Israeli unscrews the battery, the Chinaman moves off to the Park. They each say goodbye, but only to me.

"Anytime," the old man confides. "They're in the cellar."

"You buzz me when you get good cables," says the handyman.

"Would've told," says the Oriental with the dog. I call a tow truck.

At her last job Connie was assigned to the women's beat. She wrote about truffles, food processors, fluid cream moisturizers, sourdough, Parsons tables, stoneware and track lighting. She discovered little shops, ethnic originals, tucked away in the East Twenties or on Atlantic Avenue. At Christmas we still get a bag of Syrian bread from a merchant who thinks she put him on the map. She knows the family history of the Siamese grocer, the school attended by the son of the irritable Korean vegetable man (who has a Ph.D.), the province of the Indian who keeps us in tondori. She has visited the source of West Side bagels; she knows the route traveled by imported French country furniture, the history of the artichoke. But she hasn't bought anything for the apartment in a year, hates cooking and no longer remembers the best place in Paris to get *poulet de Bresse*. The money has stopped coming in; her agent thinks she's moved to Connecticut. She may never set foot in Bloomingdale's again. "No loss," she says. "Others are ready to take my place."After welcoming her to the club and observing that this is no doubt a natural stage in her development, I busy myself with supportive suggestions. "Why not politics?"

She says she has no head for the details. "I hate formal relationships. We are being squeezed to death by functionaries."

A teenager has just dropped a diet cola can in our path, and she has restrained herself from returning it to him. "Pardon me, you dropped this," is what she would usually say, while I tried to pretend I never saw her before.

"The way we treat Broadway says something about our public life."

"Historic preservation?"

"Ten applicants for every job. Dribs and drabs of federal money.

"Publishing?"

"Nobody edits anymore."

"Filmmaking?"

"Come on."

"Could it be, old girl, that one might say you don't want to solve this problem?"

For dramatic effect she picks up a candy bar wrapper and tosses it into a carton near the fruit stand. "I'm not liking people these days. They're stuck in their ruts. That's no different than it ever was, but I'm no longer interested. I know everyone too well."

Then we should get out—a new shuffle. But to where? And to what? We sit around Binni's kitchen, offering some social misery after her consulting-room day of serious professional misery. Her contribution, offered between cleaver whacks at a clove of garlic, is that we live on a merry-go-round. "Simplify, reduce, focus." Frustrated by perpetually suspending judgment, by having to take patients as they are, her off-hours voice takes a stand: "Accept, resign, adjust." An orange cat leaps to the counter and claws the bluefish—whack—only to scamper down in fright. Presently Binni's excellent Montrachet dulls the edge.

"I should have lived in another age." Connie is wishing she was a pioneer woman in a wagon train crossing Nebraska. "In their last year before retirement, city employees who've loafed for decades suddenly start working overtime like crazy. It doubles the amount of their pensions. I have nothing against security for the elderly, but look what these rules do to people."

"When I was in the hospital last year," Binnie says, "they kept twenty-five of us waiting in a drafty basement for chest x-rays. Some of the patients looked terminal. I told the nurse I didn't need a chest x-ray, but she said it had to be done in case I sued them."

"Instead of standards," Connie says angrily, "we have rules—rules instead of respect. This whole litigious pile of crap. I'm beginning to sound like Ronald Reagan."

"Who did nothing about it when he was governor of California."

"Maybe his intentions weren't honorable. Gimme, gimme. Anyway, it's too big. But Binni is right. You should covet harmony, Jeremy. Delight. Perhaps there's a difference between working with laws and being responsible for them.

"That's not good enough. I need harmony in all its concreteness. D. H. Lawrence has a character who sought harmony and found it in the organization of the modern corporation."

"You won't get it by being concrete, Jeremy. But try wild columbine."

"Granny Smiths?" Binnie asks.

"I prefer Northern Spies," I answer.

"The problem with the concrete," Connie says, "is that you'll treat it as something to be used. You'll stick it in a brief. Harmony is really a transaction between a person, a thing and a field of force, and thus.... "

"Difficult to discuss."

"Right, but we should try, no matter how flaky it sounds. You know, I would have put *Howard's End* on my list of the concrete, but 'Only connect' has become a cliché. There's something in the very wheel of this life that destroys our reference points. I think that's why I wrote about soufflés. We're coming to believe that today's insight is tomorrow's old newspaper. A good soufflé never changes."

By the book on family constellations, our marriage is programmed to work. Having younger brothers, Connie knows how to take care of men, and as an only son I want something of a mother in my wife. At one point we considered separating, but once you've come to terms with it, incest makes the heart grow fonder.

"I used to think," Clare is saying, "instead of all this nonsense with proposals and long lunches and interminable meetings with earnest people asking me ridiculous questions about battered spouses or methadone, why not just say, look, buster, let's screw for the grant, and get it over with fast. Then I could go home, read the *Times* over a beer, write my briefs in daylight for a change and get on with my life. But now I have more tolerance for the style of it all. It's an art form. Anyway, they don't want to screw—though, of course, sometimes they do. What I'm getting at is, why destroy the theater of it? What would be left? They're plenty involved when they ask how come the Legal Aid Society isn't representing these people or complain about their budget cuts and how the stock market decline is turning philanthropy sour. But then they go back to their glittery cages, where nobody has ever paid for a personal call, where vacations start with free air fare to a conference on judicial administration at the Del Coronado, or some such nonsense. They go back, have a meeting where the really important thing is whether they owe a favor to somebody on our board, and the next most important thing is whether some organization—God, I hate that word—with the power to embarrass them is behind what we want to do. Screwing for a grant would give up all that control—and with control, esteem, because after all, they're deciding which good works are good and work.

"I've come to realize, at least to accept, that winning at this game is probably my greatest gift. Now I'm enjoying the whole routine. When they stop asking questions, raising problems, pondering budgets out loud, I sneak in a few more doubts about my own grant—just a few shafts, mind you, because these people are sharp, quick and totally composed. Unless they're dealing with a black militant or an Indian brave or some butch feminist; then they sweat. They're careful not to see these people except under very structured conditions—that is, three foundation types to each potential troublemaker. But I let them know I don't think I have a right to a grant until it clears an impartial evaluation. That proves we're worthy, you see. That we want, that we expect them to take care; that it's their duty to us as well as themselves to hire two Columbia professors to talk to our clients, accountants, advisory committee, even the people we sue. And saying this—with conviction, of course—makes me a member of their club. I am safe. Suddenly the money is available. In a pinch they'll even call and ask if I would, as a personal favor, put in for a grant to study when death becomes legal, the rule of law in Paraguay, or whatever's getting pushed that week."

Clare is not usually so loose. The grass must have oiled her brain. I find it interesting that she calls the sexual act screwing, because when she goes to court she is like a screw being tightened. Her skin taut, with pushed-back hair making her particularly vulnerable, her thoughts outrush words from her brain. She twists paper clips, crumples envelopes, raps the lectern with her knuckles. Then, aware suddenly, as if caught with a finger in her nose, she slows the nervous pace and substitutes a deliberate, monotonous, simple explanation. For a moment the driven quality is gone, replaced by its opposite; she is talking to a child. Eventually, picking up speed, she is back to normal hysteria. During this performance the room is still, a beach without surf. Judges find it impossible to cope with her body language. They come off the bench mopping their brows and taking deep breaths. Poor fellow, I thought, watching one who swept off to his chambers with a dazed look, the only sex he sees down here is rape cases.

When I look at the art world for insight, my empirical, though highly impressionistic research is not auspicious. Pictures in Susan's loft speak differently to the artist who made them than to the viewer. In me they produce frustration with an outwardness I am unable to penetrate. Instead of insight I gather outsight. Kit paints bottles, the result of an evolution through camels, dots, squiggles and bones. He worries that a new star on the horizon, apparently into sea glass, will horn in. Susan paints lace, but her dealer wants her to do cows. "Changing from columns to stripes can be traumatic," Susan says, referring to a colleague. "You may get a reputation."

The most abiding problem I have with New York is the need to explain it. We are stuck here but must be ready with a civil answer why, one that preserves our dignity and freedom of choice. Lately we have been ennobled by endurance.

Aimless, and therefore irritable, I bitch at Annie. On a case she and I rarely talk about differences. We go with what we have, taking up our places at the intersection of law and client, oblivious to other paths that could be taken. Without this focus, we might be lost. But when there is a mutual wish to fight, the battle assumes an ideological cast, turning on her rebellion and my resignation. Brushing dopey bangs from her eyes, she demands small, decentralized structures, community control, organizing the clients. I will talk too much about monster class-action suits. Even scaled down as we are, recognizing the failure of anything that smacks of adventure, these abstractions are dangerous. In any situation she will find the people with the greatest, most unmeetable needs; she is a Magellan of the double bind. What I find hopeless gets her high.

"You are, old lady, the embodiment of everything that's excellent in do-goodism, but the tribe is doomed, done in by cost-benefit analysis and zero-based budgeting. The only rule I've been able to extract is that the rich get richer. Without something to start with, you're wasting your time."

"Biological determinist bullshit." Unfortunately, Annie isn't really angry; she sees that I'm just letting off steam and knows too well my typical escape routes. She gets really upset only when forced to rely on reasoned argument.

I try again, weakly. "You feel responsible for the world."

Once this would arouse her to plunge into Family Court like a fullback diving for short yardage. Her kids—her clients—are trapped; they can only be placed in an unconscionable institution or returned to an impossible home. For Annie, there is always a better solution.

"Most people sympathize with the victims, but you, a typical product of American legal education—you get angry at them. Arrogant and selfish as ever, Jeremy."

We are both right.

Perhaps an international boondoggle will freshen the breeze.

I know that the visa application necessary for my trip is routine because the helpful Miss Kirner tells me so four times. "It's only a form," she says. I wonder whether she is one of them, or merely a nice girl from Woodmere hired to weed out dangerous travelers. "We check *all* permits with the Department of Interior in Pretoria when lectures are involved. It will only take six weeks. We'll send it out in the diplomatic pouch today." She sits behind a two-inch-thick wall of shatterproof glass. When I tell her I'll be difficult to reach in six weeks, she agrees to check with the consul but returns in a jiffy with his regrets. "It's only routine. Nothing personal, you understand."

The pilot welcomes us aboard in English. Somewhere over the Gulf of Guinea, he switches to Afrikaans. My first day in Johannesburg, still confused after seventeen hours aloft, I take a before-breakfast run through the streets of a suburb called Houghton. High on a plateau, lumbering along in the thin air, passing children in school uniforms and black newsboys hawking papers at traffic signals, the cars so clean they look driven from the showroom, I turn down a lane of walled villas. Gates are still shut tight against the night, flowers cascade into the street. A black domestic in a kerchief and faded housedress hobbles toward me down the road. I am an inept but jolly runner, knowing that nothing in the day to come can approach the pain of four torturous miles, pressing my body to behave. To my fleeting good morning, she replies, "Good morning, master."

"So…." The only comment of the internationally known author and essayist. She seems to be saying "Naïve American" in that defensive way of educated Europeans dealing with the unclassified, treating Americans as if we were characters out of Henry James or had never witnessed a man robbed with a fountain pen. I have not seen her for five years, but nothing has changed. Twelve thousand miles away we had lunched on West Fifty-sixth Street. She was coming up for air, and as a proper host I thought to regale her with local color.

My friend Charley was a criminal defense lawyer who worked for practically nothing in the dingiest parts of the catacomb and lived alone in a loft, eating too much peanut butter. A life out of Dickens. I hoped the literary allusion would please, but her lips merely puckered at the disappointing wine. I persevered. Charley loved his car, an old Mustang convertible with a book value of two hundred fifty dollars. One night at three A.M. he got a call from the cops. His car has been found; come and get it.

"I didn't know it was lost."

"Not lost, stolen. Get it out of our driveway."

Charley threw on a pair of pants, tied his sneakers in the cab and showed up at the precinct house to find the cop and the car thief arguing.

"You never told me my rights," said the thief.

"I did so," said the cop.

"You did not."

"I did so."

"Hold on," Charley intervened. "Even though you probably stole my car, I'll tell you your rights." And he repeated the litany. "You don't have to talk; you can have a lawyer at state expense. Blah, blah. Got it?"

"Now, look," the man said. "I didn't take your car, I was just sitting in it for a friend. But supposing I did steal it—what good will it do to send me downtown? If I pull three months on Rikers, the landlord will take my things for rent. I'll be back on the street at Christmas time, broke, with no clothes. What'll I do? Steal a car, of course."

Charley grabbed the thief's yellow sheet and confirmed that he meant what he said. He had a dozen arrests for unauthorized use of motor vehicles.

Charley liked cops, hated prosecutors and knew a good plea for mercy when he heard one. He was about to take his car and split when the thief overplayed his hand.

"Besides, why would anyone bother with your heap?" Here was a consummate rascal, one who lifted a treasure only to degrade it.

Charley inspected the car. It was wounded beyond repair; top slashed, gears stripped, ignition pried apart with a screwdriver. He was furious, and resolved to press charges, quite forgetting the presumption of innocence. But when he got to court the next day the case was before a mean and incompetent judge, a man who carried a gun under his robe, who never practiced law, who was appointed as a payoff for years as a court clerk. The defense attorney had never tried a case; more important, he didn't know a plea bargain from a search warrant. Brother to brother, the prosecutor promised Charley a special effort. "We'll offer him eleven months on a plea; otherwise he can wait for trial with the homicides."

The seesaw shifted back; Charley didn't know what to do. But when the case was called he had to intervene—he leaped up, brushed aside the defense lawyer, glared at the DA and told the judge that as the complainant he wanted to report a serious miscarriage of justice. His buddy, the defendant, always had permission to borrow the car.

The case was dismissed, but Charley was still fuming about the loss of his beloved Mustang. He went back to his office, wrote up the story just as it happened, sold it as a life-in-our-town feature to the Sunday *News* for seven hundred dollars and made a down payment on a BMW with a sun roof.

"So...."

At the workers' aid clinic in Johannesburg, the talk over tea and milk is about what a law student named Geoffrey calls "the latest Russian-novel case." He runs it down. Jerad Malat, age twenty-three, he thinks. Address: John Vorster Square, the glass-box lockup near the motorway. Charge: illegal entry. Punishment: deportation. Prognosis: grim.

Malat claims he was born near Riverlea, a colored township on the outskirts of Jo'burg. At an early age his sailor father took him to Egypt. They lived in Cairo until Jerad was old enough to join his father at sea. But last spring the old man died, and Jerad, returning to South Africa through Mozambique to find his mother, was picked up by a border patrol looking for terrorists near Swaziland. The clinic has contacted the mother, who denies maternity. But she has been reclassified as an Indian and is probably afraid that by acknowledging a coal-black son she will end up on a tribal reservation. There are no records of his birth, according to Geoffrey; however, Jerad knows things that only a son would know. The Afrikaaners want to deport him, but the Egyptians refuse to take him back, claiming he's a South African. The Bantu administrator, the white who tells blacks where to live, can't pack him off to a rural homeland because there is no proof of tribal affiliation. Malat has been sitting in jail for six months on an open commitment. Geoffrey is keen on games, especially cricket. He seems very young and lean, light as whipped cream, and complains of being unused to this sort of responsibility. "If I were to die," he says, "no one would know Malat's story. He might never get out."

I am not prepared for the countryside. Lion and elephant roaming remote game parks were apparently expected to show up hard by suburban shopping centers. In its emptiness the veld is as vast as the sky. Downtown Johannesburg could be Cleveland; Durban feels like a British Miami Beach. The brown hills remind me of California in summer. This is low-budget Africa, shot in the unconvincing mountains behind San Bernadino, beautiful but domesticated. Despite a steely resolve to avoid false analogy, I have been here before. The issues come in different packages, but like name brands in a supermarket they are essentially the same.

At cocktails before my first lecture, the publisher who is my host confides quietly that he should leave while there is still time but can't bring himself to. "The good life, you know." I have a passel of such conversations, each private; whites trapped by their swimming pools, prisoners on a tennis court. I wonder about the Jews who left Germany and those who remained: what distinguished them? When the American embassy holds a qualification exam for doctors who wish to emigrate, three hundred show up. My host predicts bitterly that they'll all settle in Beverly Hills. "It's impossible to get a doctor these days. I know a woman who was being wheeled into the operating room for major surgery. Just before the anesthesiologist put her out, he told her there would be a different surgeon attending. Her doctor had left for good on the morning plane."

While I'm waiting to speak, chatting with the guests and sipping Cape sherry, we learn the security branch trucked a comatose Steve Biko a thousand miles across the country the day before he died. Afraid of his revolutionary potential, they shoved him naked into the back of a van. The word is that Biko's autopsy will identify massive brain damage as the cause of death. "No doubt," says a black reporter for the *World*, "the police will claim that he fell down a flight of stairs or slipped in the shower. You know, of course, that we have the cleanest prisoners in all of Africa because they take so many showers."

Lulu, an American stringer straight out of Columbia Journalism School, joins us. She is wearing a red jersey, khaki jeans and white tennis shoes; all the other women in the room are dressed in skirts. "These people," she says, one American to another, "had everything going for them—gold, diamonds, climate—and they've thrown it away."

When he hears of my mission, the black reporter moves toward the bar. "The days of legal defense are over" is his parting shot. (The reporter was arrested, his home searched, his editor detained, his paper closed a month after I left.) Lulu tells me American journalists who once covered Vietnam have begun arriving in droves, no doubt smelling blood.

When the committee of lawyers sits down to plan strategy, I'm right at home with the apocalyptic mood and wan jokes about bugging. Despite the agitated talk of would-be lawsuits and hoped-for exposés, the group is pessimistic. It strikes me that once we go to court Rudy and I always assume victory—it's second nature to us—whereas these people expect defeat. "When we accomplish something, they just pass a law and take it back. But they do it by the book, mind you. If they want to authorize the police to hang a black by the toes, they'll put a bill through parliament."

"How about this new one regulating the flow of foreign currency for charitable purposes?"

"It's intended to keep out political money from the States, but it also says we have to register a church bazaar or a Red Cross bake sale. You see, the Nationalists observe the forms. We are a people of laws. I think you Americans call it procedural justice."

In the mirror of these men, my peers, I sneak a look at my image. My lot is infinitely superior. The works here have been covered with grease, which has been allowed to set. The parts are now frozen and won't move. My colleagues around the table take mallets and chisels to the clotted muck but only chip slivers. It is futile. The blades break, but with the handles they keep on pounding. They must do it to keep alive, to know that despite everything one is a good person.

A common dilemma. These liberals are stuck with their obedience to laws that are unjust. If in this country we are able to wriggle off horns on which the South Africans are impaled, it is because a higher law, the Constitution, offers the hope of ultimate resurrection. The blessing is not that a two-hundred-year-old document devised by the gentry to govern a few million fishermen and farmers really settled anything—indeed, very little—or that the Framers were men of high principle who abjured logrolling and back scratching. Not a bit. The terms of the Constitution are deeply flawed, but the *idea* of a constitution is as perfect as tongue can tell. Arrangements handed down from outside our time and place, like values absorbed invisibly in childhood, endure—if anything endures, that is. These arrangements or goals or ends, and the daily way in which they are bent, tested and restored, are the only god left. It is the freedom to bend that counts most; this is our liberty. We dispute God's *works*, tamper with the fittings, fiddle with history, ineptly turn the general to the specific. We are lazy, selfish, lustful and foolish. But the ends are let be. There are exceptions. My God allows for them; in a process that depends on lawyers, there will always be exceptions. Law is a course of, something that commands, a rule, a question of, experience, not logic. We resist, break, fear, enforce and obey it. The law is both made and given. Pity is the virtue of.

The Woman on the 747

THE FIRST TIME I saw Baker after his release from prison he looked as pulled together as the tight-fitting second skin of his sky-blue jumpsuit. Between helpings of crisp chicken and overcooked vegetables, dished out at a soul-food restaurant near what used to be the West Side docks, he asked if his conviction would keep him from going to law school. Choking on a bone, I wondered where it all came from, this world of would-be esquires. Baker ignored my coughing fit and told Connie of his months in prison: "Plenty of energy among the inmates, but it peters out in petty haggling. The black dudes and the Spanish take it out on each other, or they hassle the guards. A lot of domestic squabbling. TV's the biggest change since I was a kid; now we're locked up with cartoons and game shows. But, you know, I'm glad I was there. I'd forgotten what it was like. I was gettin' kinda distracted."

Connie astonished me by putting it to him straight. "Jeremy has been tossing in his sleep over this for months," she said. "Was the seizure real or a put-on?"

Baker's years on the streets of Harlem had prepared him for anything, even the graduate degree in assertiveness training of this well-proportioned and overbred white woman. Without missing a forkful of poisonous-looking black beans, he answered as if she'd simply asked for change of a quarter. "The best I can tell, it was induced by the circumstances. You might say I was disposed to it—it seemed the thing to do—but I didn't rightly pretend."

"You don't know yourself?"

"You probably think I killed the firebugs, too, and I could have—back a ways, I could have. Now I just work with what people give me. Kids sometimes take the law in their hands like that to thank us for the absolutely perfect world we've turned over to them. A mistake, but what can you do? And it stops fires. So I exploited it. Now that I'm in administration, I squeeze things for the juice."

"Could that explain the heart attack?"

"And there was your husband."

"My husband?"

129

"He needed a break. I thought he was gonna bust the judge and ruin himself."

After dinner we walked to the car, left in a perfectly legal parking space, one of the few in the city. Gone. Hoisted away by some tow-truck jockey who hadn't met his daily quota. I was about to rant, my shoulders stooped in the utter defeat of urban man, but Baker only howled. He leaned back from the waist and threw his head to the sky; out flashed his huge palms. "There's no way you gonna beat this city. My, my, no way, but you'll keep trying anyway." The howls became general, and louder still we sang dirty songs all the way to the pound, where for fifty bucks, cash ("no checks, no credit"), the surly cop on duty returned our wheels.

I am not making progress with life choices. Something has gone wrong with the program. As long as I was basically a good boy and marched just enough out of step to call attention to myself, there was the promise that by this time of life I'd be ready to take command. Slade's call, these job offers, should be relished, slithered on the tongue like fettuccine Alfredo. But the law is simply too vast, thinking about its nature and my place in its cosmology empties me of energy, saps my confidence. Still, I must come to terms, or at least be ready in case Dee wants to know what her father's life is about or Studs Terkel should stop in, tape recorder slung over his shoulder, asking what goes on here. So I play the fool, the blindfolded man in the old joke whose sense of the elephant is the trunk, thigh or tail. After a number of years groping around the beast, I now tell myself some reckoning is necessary, no matter how unsatisfactory.

The law is supposed to make us better than we are, to keep us from grabbing what we can through stealth, chicanery or muscle. Law exists to sap our strength, to keep us from acting ourselves. Revenge, you see, is bad for business, and agentry, while secondhand and expensive, calms the passions and cools the blood. Once this vicarious quality was enough to cause people to give the whole apparatus a wide berth, but now we cherish our access to judges; they have been saddled with choices no one else wants to make, risks no one wants to carry. Let the courts define the space between abortion and murder, privacy and information; let *them* take the knife and cut the pie.

In return, judges are granted a certain immunity. It doesn't strike me as unusual that so far they have only rarely been the targets of assassination. Now, lawyers: you might expect it would be different with lawyers; they have no robes and throne. Revolutionaries advertise that lawyers will go first, but few of them have been hit. The explanation, I think, is that lawyers also are judges. They stick facts in boxes and label them, tell us what the law encourages, insists upon, permits; they are priests who translate oracular jargon into fashion and cliché, fitting the round peg of today's fact into the square hole of yesterday's law. What does this part of the animal do to us? Lawyers are given—and have taken—power, but it isn't fully acknowledged. We let them make these choices, but we're not happy about it. We complain but are docile. They run our lives and we are ambivalent about it. But so are the lawyers, whether they admit it or not. They hold forth from on high without a clue, most of the time, as to what the damned oracle is saying. They have a false self.

"Let's face it," Clare says, tired of this talk, "you're becoming a type, the middle-aged hippie, though you're neither as old nor as loose as the name implies." She's attacking me to demonstrate that she no longer needs a mentor. "Middle-aged hippies sometimes leave their spouse and run off with youth, but just as often they're family men and women. If they're separated, you're likely to find them living two blocks from their kids. They spend a lot of time with their children. They're the fathers you see waiting to pick up Junior at a gymnastics or dance class. They may get heavily into drugs, but more often the addiction is to bean sprouts and brown rice. On the West Side middle-aged hippies are almost a majority. The clan rides the subway after nine A.M., wearing washed-out jeans, work shirts and corduroy jackets The women have marvelous braided, graying hair. As well as I can piece it together, the mainspring is a fussiness with external restraint; they're trying to stay in the world but not be of it, to stay on a payroll but work odd hours, to live off investments without just clipping coupons, to not have to deal with people on terms they don't like. If they have anything to do with corporations, they're consultants. They dream of an independent income, not to buy things but to be free of submitting to the forms. They aren't lazy; in fact, planning books, plays and campaigns is a mark of the breed. But they jump around from one thing to the next, and when you come right down to it I don't trust them."

Fritz's recurring idea that I give up the law to write thrillers sounds preposterous, but that doesn't mean it won't work. Wild ideas of this sort keep the city from going under. That a project has the backing of an established agent with a track record of putative successes will see it through and provide enough momentum to sustain the mirage for a profitable season. By next year another illusion will be ready for market. Speaking of markets, Wall Street itself may be such a creature, surviving because enough people are able to deceive themselves about its necessity.

As Binni's legal adviser I must truck with her investment counselor, the impeccable Mr. Prunty, who comes to New York from Philadelphia only to buy what he calls colored stones at Sotheby Parke Bernet.

For years Mr. Prunty has been shifting his more adventurous clients to the Swiss franc, gold bullion and private real-estate arrangements honchoed by investment bankers. At his Churchillian best, he declaims that the stock market is managed not by sleazy stock manipulators but by an unconscious need to maintain the belief that its function is still vital. Capital can be raised, invested and transferred more cheaply. The brokers, banks and insurance companies keep it going up and down, up and down, in order to reassure themselves that the game isn't over. Prunty calls them sheep. When he says the word in a deep doomsday voice, as if he were announcing the end of the world on the eleven o'clock news, I actually see sheep bleating and baaing out of the IRT near William Street, waiting patiently for the elevators at Chase Manhattan Plaza. What with inflation and capital gains taxes, Prunty has given up on securities and commercial paper. Money went out of his mind long ago.

"I don't have a crystal ball," he tells Binni disarmingly, "but autographs have outperformed diamonds in Zurich. Signatures of the departed famous. An Einstein goes for a thousand now, double what it was six months ago. Right now I'm keeping my eye on Fermi and Bohr."

Mr. Prunty always takes us to the most expensive restaurant he can find in order to razz Uncle Sam, who's paying 70 percent of the bill. Studying the entrecôte maître d'hôtel, I survey a line of gristle: this much from the government, this much from him. Lapsing into antic humor after the second bottle of Mouton Rothschild, he lets slip the secret of his success: buy low and sell high.

Beating the drums that in his stable he has the best genre writer since Ambler—a combination of Conrad, Le Carré and Joyce Carol Oates—Fritz thinks he'll create such demand for my services that a few judiciously chosen chapters will hook the kind of juicy advance a publisher must protect. He is convinced that a large advance means a fat budget for ads and that promotion will ensure success.

"Of course, people can't be hyped more than seven or eight times running, but they can be misled into expecting something and then think they've gotten it. Remember, we're talking about magic. It wouldn't work if you were a fraud or a nebbish, but you're neither. You just need the right package."

Connie and I have indecisive talks about indecision. Our paths cross only when we go off in different directions. Now that I want to hire a guru consulting service to run my life, dispatching periodic reassurances the way a trust company issues monthly checks, Connie insists on doing everything herself. I want to go into receivership, and nothing is further from her mind. I know this because she's suddenly learned that the car does not automatically fill up with gas. Meanwhile I've started forgetting things: keys, address book, diary, one of those insufferable lunch meetings with politicians who broadcast the seeds of change while running for office and now have to figure out what to do. The money Fritz is after Connie thinks dirty; she also believes a judgeship will set world records in tedium. From the library she returns with a pile of books on life in neolithic Britain and suggests a walking tour of the moors. Despite stern warnings to me about the tyranny of work, she hangs in there like a good wife—whither thou goest, etc. But she's doing some judging of her own. Despite the years, she still looks at me and wonders whether she should have married a poet. I'm still a stranger, an other, a potential enemy. Out of the corner of my eye I watch back, hoping to discover something that pleases her, waiting for a sign that she thinks I've stumbled onto my own version of harmony.

Fritz offers a good cigar after a big dinner; while he nags and nudges, passivity overtakes me, I yawn and nod my head, inhaling the escape value of his fantasy. We will move to the farm; Connie can rediscover gardening; the children can learn about animals. I will take a Scottish pen name; I've always thought the Scots do this stuff best. Does Angus or Ian suit me better?

If ultimately I am calm in the face of these tugs and pulls, it is because I'm beginning to feel that whatever I do, the best of me will win out.

Which is the only explanation for suddenly starting to think about Roger. It was Roger who taught me that even the most handicapped child creates what he needs and does not have. I was ten or eleven; he was thirteen. Every Wednesday my mother made me play with him. None of her usual beating around the bush, no "It's really good for you" crap—just a conclusive "Do it." She wasn't concerned about the afternoon baseball games where I was desperately needed at the hot corner to keep Sid Gerstman from ramming line drives between third and short; she preferred results to good intentions.

Roger's condition was so ugly that in those days it hadn't been given a name. The special teacher from the Board of Ed referred to it as a rare muscular disease. Phyllis, Roger's mother, merely said he was crippled. With great effort he could move his head, arms and legs, but only a few inches at a time and so was imprisoned in a wheelchair. In the morning Phyllis carried him from bed to a chair, in late afternoon from chair to bath, and back from the chair to bed at night. She was a tiny woman with hair of steel wool tied back in a bun; lifting Roger's dead weight gave her walnut-size biceps and a spaghetti-like circuitry of veins. She held him on the potty with the muscles of a wrestler, an iron grip that I envied.

In her kitchen, which smelled of egg salad, Roger snapped out orders and honed a brain that had quickly outgrown his frail body. He was fast becoming a mathematical prodigy, but on Wednesday afternoons I saw only a sick child thirsting for a taste of the world beyond the chair. For three hours, until Phyllis came to stretch him out in an odd cast-iron tub that could have been a holding tank for dolphins, he seduced me into a world of deeds. He insisted on what he called The Game. He was never short of plots; playing on his condition and his superior age, he assigned the roles, channeled the drama. A pair of good guys hunting or hunted, a secret, dangerous mission. We would get lost in a cave, stuck in quicksand, captured by the Germans or trapped in the jungle. We played all the parts, rendering evil in falsetto or basso profundo. We wrestled mad scientists to the ground and routed dictators with Trojan horses. All women who fell into our hands were warm and voluptuous, attracted by the joy of grasping Roger's tinkler. At the crucial moment he claimed them for his own, and pity was never so near that I gave up without a fight. As the enemy closed in, I'd divert him by falling on the ground, far enough from the chair for him to see, and kick the linoleum with my feet, shouting with triumph. "Take that, you bastard. I'll show you. Zap. And that." The heavies begged forgiveness, whined, pleaded for remission; their watery eyes sought mercy from the final judge of all, reigning lordly in his wheeled throne. In the excitement, Roger's throat would gargle and wheeze. Toy fists gently punched the air, patted the Formica tray on which his elbows rested. About to pronounce judgment, down they flew. Raised like a drawbridge, down again. Death. Death to vermin. His chest heaved with congestion, his breath hacking its way out, cutting through mucus. Phyllis sat smoking on the back stoop, her thoughts far away, until the sound of gagging reached her. The glass of the door jiggled as she slammed it against the breeze from the bay. She drew him forward and massaged his lungs, her face buried in his back.

Roger inert, a slug in a saucer of beer, straining at the slope, then falling back, occupies the same cell of stirring memory as Lenny Bruce. At a critical moment in a short life, the comic seer discharged his lion of the bar and prepared to finish the battle himself with the criminal law. 1 was sent down to Greenwich Village by a mutual friend to give him on-the-job training. He sat cross-legged on an army cot that masqueraded as a bed at the Earle Hotel. He was hemmed in by treatises on the law, trial transcripts and tapes of the allegedly obscene performances that had led the People of the State of New York, as the prosecutor kept reminding him, to settle accounts for blaspheming in a coffeehouse.

Though not condoned, in primitive societies murder is viewed as a matter that primarily concerns individuals and their kin. The death penalty is reserved for blasphemy, by which heathen lawmakers mean a crime that rends the social contract and thumbs its nose at parochial gods. Despite the lofty origins of his offense, and though famous for flights of irreverence and incongruity, Bruce was respectful as only a layman can be: for me, "da lore"; for him, "The Law." When faced with words in a statute book, he imagined granite tablets. This man who made his living by revealing his private stream of conjunctions felt it necessary to document every assertion; he could topple all idols but this one. He kept reaching for the books, reading aloud until even the traffic on Eighth Street seemed to notice, his voice trailing off at the unaccustomed parenthetical clauses and dangling modifiers. In disgust and frustration he'd toss a book back on the pile, the mass of flotsam shifting on the soft mattress. Tapes unraveled. In a chair at the foot of the bed sat a cool blonde, a volunteer secretary—hell, a complete service industry—awaiting dictation from a boss who'd forgotten she was there.

He was fascinated by the text and took it literally. The courts of the United States have jurisdiction to enjoin denial of constitutional rights. His rights to speech, assembly and association had been violated. Therefore the courts of the United States had the power to order the chief prosecutor, Frank Hogan, to kennel his dogs.

"But there's a rule that says a federal judge can't interfere with a state criminal prosecution. Besides—"

"Where? Show it to me."

"In the annotation, the pocket part in the back of the book."

His eyes blinked rapidly; he was probably stoned.

For his formal sentencing I set him straight. I persuaded him to give up trying to imitate Perry Mason and simply make the law part of *his* act. It was my only contribution to a brilliant performance. One judge had been for him—though only on constitutional grounds—but remained disgusted at the ribaldry. Of the two who branded him a pornographer and voted to convict, one was uncomprehending; he ground his teeth, confronted with this lunatic. But the other, a black man, dug it all; his eyes glistened, he suppressed laughter, he loved the routine. He understood, and for a moment I almost believed Lenny would bring him out of his role into humanity, which in this case meant a vote for probation. But when the show was over the score was two-one for a jail term. Still, at least Bruce had gone down as himself, which is the most anyone can ask.

On the phone Sam tells me it's just that I peaked early. "Don't expect any sympathy with the costs of success. Eighty percent of the world is starving, ninety-nine percent of it is empty. Face it, you're wanted." He's saying, "Stop agonizing and be grateful for it," when an unexpected visitor fills up my doorway and looks over my head as if in place of my little cube she expects a vast auditorium filled with hundreds. I wave her in, tell Sam to go back to counting neutron bombs and hang up.

She has an enormous face and big, broad shoulders. Hoops dangle from her ears. Her breasts are gourds. The black of her jersey sets off huge freckles. The afro is so close it must have been trimmed in the elevator. She literally yanks a scraggly, unshaven white man into the room and pushes him into a chair. Shades droop almost to his chin. With a smack of her lips and a lightning stroke she removes the files from the other chair and dumps them on my desk.

"At last, a real lawyer."

"At last?"

"I tell you, we've been run ragged with you all, and this time I don't want no more of it. I ain't going nowhere." Digging out her cigarettes, she offers them around with the air of a proud hostess. We all light up.

"Now that the show biz is over, what can I do to help?"

She doesn't waste words. "I got a Rockefeller drug charge. Never been to jail and don't plan to start now." "How did you get here?"

"Well, at Civil Liberties they sent me to Constitutional Rights, and they sent me to Kramer, and he wants four thou and I ain't got it. Kibbe doesn't, either. He's a musician and hasn't worked in six months. No, just shut up, Kibbe; you done one gig in Jersey City and that don't count." Kibbe is making a microscopic investigation of my floor and hasn't threatened a word. "At the clinic they only do welfare and landlord-tenant; they said you were their criminal man."

"I'm semiretired. Teaching. I take very few cases."

"Ain't this a law school? Where you gonna get a lawyer if not in a school for lawyers?"

"Let's cut some red tape. What have they got you for?" In contrast to her gala entrance, she is suddenly quiet.

"It's a long story."

"The charge?"

"Sale of cocaine."

"How much?"

"An ounce."

"Do you want him here?"

"Sure. We're a team.... when he's awake."

"Is he involved?"

"No. They did it at my place. I work where I live, and the customers wouldn't like him around."

"What do you do?"

"Dominatrix."

"Anything else?"

"That's it."

"Do you specialize?"

"No, the whole number. Whips, sticks, body work. I like to work with my hands."

"Look, I haven't decided to represent you. I probably can't. Let me hear more, and if I can't I'll try to find someone who can. Whatever you tell me—"

"Is strictly confidential, and you'll only tell it to everybody you meet on the way home tonight."

"What makes you think that?"

"How often do you meet a dominatrix? I'm an interesting person. Everybody says that."

"Tell him the story, Ginny." Kibbe is alive.

"I have a steady clientele. Work out of my place. Sixty-fifth and First. No funny business. I'm saving to get out. Kibbe and I, we're gonna get out of Manhattan. I send money to my mother. Okay, a while back I get a customer offers me a deal on coke. He says there's no way he can get rid of it. Came into his hands from a sailor friend. I shoulda known better. Most of my customers are businessmen. This fellow didn't fit in. Spanish."

"Get to the point, Ginny."

"Shut up, dope." She says it mildly. "You shouldn't get it wrong. We don't always fight."

"I understand."

"How could you understand? Anyway, I tell him I'm no dealer, but the bastard says keep the stuff around and one of your johns will want it. Pay when you peddle it. So I don't say nothing and he leaves it with me. A week later I get another first-timer who comes in wanting something screwy like ice cubes on his prick. I give it to him and then he asks if I have any stuff. I tell him to look in a drawer. He finds it and grabs me on a drug bust. At Constitutional Rights they say it was entrapment, but they're busy."

"What happened in court?"

"They gave me bond for five hundred, and this paper."

She fumbles in her satchel and hands me an indictment folded like a handkerchief. While I read it she takes in the clutter. I wonder whether it makes her think I'm busy or disorganized.

It's Kibbe's turn. "Look, we don't want charity. We'll pay you off. Just give us time."

"Can't." "Why?" "It's against my religion and the rules of the clinic. We don't take paying customers."

He's skeptical, but lets it drop. "What's her exposure?"

"It depends on how they end up grading it. On the face of the charge, fifteen to life, but it's always reduced to a minimum of six or a year, depending. She's charged with sale of an ounce, but if she agrees to plead they'll cut it to possession, or possession with intent to sell."

"But I didn't ask for money."

"Under the law a sale is any transfer of a controlled substance. If you'd given it as a birthday present to your mother, you'd still be in the same situation. In New York sale of one-eighth of an ounce of cocaine is more serious than rape or arson. They can hold you for life. But that's what they say, not what they do. What they do is a crap game."

"Will you take my case?"

"No."

"Why?"

"Yes."

"What?"

"Tell me about your record."

"Forging a government check. Probation." Again she dives into the bag. "A few things as a kid. Here, I wrote it out. I know what you fellas want."

Kibbe is still studying the floor. "What will you do?" "We can take the edge off by slowing them down with motions and hope they lose interest. We can bargain on the charge and see what they offer, but if you don't like it we can put the cop on the stand with his story and make him look dirty. But if you lose at trial, you lose big; if we bargain—well, she'll have to do time. Maybe a year."

Ginny is quiet. Kibbe looks like a mourner. She slaps his arm. "We almost broke loose, old man. Don't worry. This is a Jewish fella, he'll get us off."

"The weakness here is the narcs," I say, wanting to give them some hope. "We might try coming out angry, as if we don't care what happens. Then the cop may get forgetful, but they'll have to save face; they may hit you with something trivial, like illegal use of a whip,. Was anything else taken besides the cocaine?"

"Naw."

The way she says it, eyes darting from my face, tells me there was something else. I decide to put off pressing her.

Clare is testy: I have no business taking the case, and Ginny falls on the wrong side of her good-woman line. Besides, there are better things to do with my time; instead of representing a battered female, I'm joining forces with one who batters. Clare is struggling to maintain control of the caseload, to set what she calls litigation priorities, and here I go again taking on a client simply because she appeared at my office. It screws up the planning, and she won't let it go without making me suffer. Clare's problem is not lack of sympathy for criminals, but the costs of my inability to say no. My clients become friends, characters in my chronicle. "You just like to play daddy," Clare says. But what can she do? Gossip that I'm taking fees or getting a little SM on the side? Tell the Soft Killer, with whom she is a strange bedfellow, that I'm no longer a workaholic?

To make matters worse, Ginny's story definitely does not have a happy ending, Our first interview drained all the humor. It turns out that the detective snatched her book of johns; Ginny steadfastly refuses to cooperate with the state, confiding that if she talks about her customers, her muscular body will soon be floating in the river or lying in the trunk of a burnt-out wreck in the Meadowlands. The DA refuses to bargain. A certain ruthlessness directs the case through the courts. By ill luck, in another case the Supremes throw cold water on a bunch of hot constitutional claims that I've raised on Ginny's behalf. When he testifies at trial, the cop comes across as having a perfect memory, looks like a choirboy and declines to offer a witness-stand confession that he planted the cocaine. The jury refuses to buy entrapment, and Ginny is stomped with six years to life in Bedford Hills. Kibbe disappears before the appeal. Free on bail, Ginny sinks to hailing cars from the doorway of a Daitch on Broadway.

I am not used to losing so many cases. Another sign of the times. The law is so dense, I once believed, that no conviction can withstand a dedicated defense—that there is always an argument, always a refinement of criminal procedure, if you look and appeal often enough. My illusion finally shatters with Ginny's case. But I did all I could. There are no regrets.

My wrangles with Clare are serious, but they don't compare to the problem of the man at the dinner party—at every dinner party I attend these days. He describes himself—or herself, if he's a she—as a no-longer-guilty former white liberal. Usually he's been mugged, or has a kid whose bike has been stolen, or thinks the city university has gone to the dogs. With their interest in creative tension, hostesses always seem to seat him within earshot of me.

When people say they sympathize, they usually mean they don't, but I really *do* sympathize with the man at the dinner party. Really. I've been mugged, and I didn't like it—especially as the mugger was not Mr. Sammler's overpowering black with a prick as long as a pike, but a runty adolescent (I placed his origins in Sunnyside) who stuck in my back what felt like a gun (I never saw it) while I was pissing in the Good Works men's room. I also share the new-found happiness of the man at the dinner party that he no longer has to *should* himself into writing checks, marching on Washington, or whatever form of expression he chose in 1968. Too much *shoulding* is bad for people.

What I do object to—so strongly that sometimes I even give in to the wishes of the hostess that a memorable incident grace her salon—is the tone of bitterness that colors the man at the dinner party's reflections on urban living. *They* are ruining something of *ours*. He is, you see, a believer in personal responsibility, not as a precept of moral philosophy, a norm to which humanity ought to aspire, but as a fact. And I am not. It makes no difference to him—even though he might say it does—that he would look at things differently if he were black. He dismisses too lightly what he owes. He jogs down Central Park's gracefully undulating paths and thinks himself a fine fellow; he is responsible for all this—never mind that Olmsted and Vaux battled Boss Tweed to keep him from turning their greensward vision into an uptown version of Chambers Street.

In my built-in feud with Clare I am less clear where I stand. Once we leave behind the curbstone Freud side of our relationship (her unwillingness to be daddied, as she calls it, and my retort that she sees a parent to rebel against in every idea she hasn't thought of first), we get to what lawyers in their haughty way call the merits. Our dispute turns on my reverence for personal history, the lengths I will go to enjoy myself as I am and will be, the only child's owner-manager relationship to himself. Clare quite rightly demands that the clinic operate by plan. In the selection of bureaucrats to harass, targets for suit, constitutional rights to assert, she correctly perceives that the tried-and-true, case-by-case, one-on-one, trial-and-error, incremental and ad hoc methods of the past don't get the job done; that once you regard inequality as solely an individual matter you've thrown in the towel. To lavish professional skill on the weak and cornered is one thing; to expect your attentions to break the grinder that turns them out is quite another.

Having thought on these matters with care, hunched over a yellow pad in the graveyard silence of her overpriced, closet-like brownstone flat, radiating her straight-from-the-ashram asceticism while Marx and Allen Ginsberg beam down hirsute approval, Clare drafts midnight memoranda urging that for once we identify our goals, the resources available to attain them, the obstacles in our path, and get the hell moving. To prod us along, the next morning she slaps down on my desk slick Xerox copies of her vision of the future. She lives for this moment (her private life having shrunk to the size of a pea), and the guidelines are exemplary. Here and there we argue over what should come first—my push for prisons competing with her affinity for women in trouble—but when she, Rudy and I meet at the office to map out our work life for next year we'll soon settle these petty differences. In dealing with the world outside the clinic, we're united by seeing ourselves in each other. Fighting outsiders, we hang together like a bunch of grapes; a consensus forms from our shared conception of the enemy. It is when we must face the implementation of Clare's well-tuned plan, the how-to-do-it, that I fail her, and probably myself as well. Over this and that, we turn bitter and rancorous.

If I try to imagine myself servant to Clare's rules, escapist fantasies overwhelm me. Stuffing cigarettes in my mouth like pretzels, I twitch at the neatly typed agenda, scratch at my dandruff, rub my crotch and daydream about my funeral. She wants me to be "objective," but out there in the grand world of political generalization I have no policy—at least, none that words will express. Those faddish ones I might safely adopt would ring canned and false, especially to Rudy and Clare, the kind of talk that leads me to cover my face when I hear it from others. Clare finds my reservations scandalous, even insincere. "You can do what you want to do," she insists. "You are not a handicapped person. This is all an underhanded way of maintaining the status quo." She will not allow me to be jagged and unpredictable.

But she's missed the point—my point, anyway, if not *the* point. I like the one-on-one; I like myself best then, and I'm entitled to that. Everyone is. Trial and error seduces me, despite its massive inefficiencies and social costs, because craft is nothing if it doesn't share my incongruities. Life yearns for fresh eccentricities. As I organize myself through work, all parts of me must be represented.

By this time Clare is shouting that I'm a lazy, reactionary, posturing hedonist. My eyes widen in fury, and I consider reaching across the table to strangle her. Rudy rises from his chair and puts his hands into the void between us, trying to make peace. A student interviewing a client in one of the cubicles across the hall comes to the door and sheepishly asks us to quiet down. I am insensitive, unhearing, brimming with rage, enjoying it. "Listen, Clare," I say, my voice vibrating with such demon strength that she has no choice. "I am free to pick my clients—for any reason or for no reason. That's how I read the Code of Professional Responsibility. I won't give up my craziness for your system, even if it's better than mine."

"Jeremy, where is your theory?"

"I don't operate by theory. Nothing's worse than bad theory. Do you hear? Fuck your theory: even if it's better than mine."

Clare sticks out her tongue in triumph. She must suppose that this is a last gasp, the theatrical screams of a general being dragged to the peace table. She's right, of course; to beat the system we need one ourselves, one that works. A good theory demands suppression and some element of self-sacrifice. That's how we must proceed—next time. But can a middleman like me, who believes his own history must be part of his work, who cares more about the process than the result, be counted on?

Though I've never collected legal fees, I know the pleasures they signify by the occasional receipt of a present from one of my clients. It's usually the losers who feel they must make amends for the trouble they've caused me, having taken up, they are sure, my valuable time in an unsuccessful effort. As the law was wrongly applied, or unjust to begin with, and I am a man of the law, my pain at the failure of the magic must equal their own. Usually, I can only drink those gifts of fealty given in defeat. Several years ago, however, one of my clients—an English teacher, of all things—mailed me a novel about Africa, unsuitably inscribed (he went to jail) "The best is yet to come." His gift was unexpected, and all the more touching since he'd been so ill-used by the professions, including my own. I was proud that Satch (as I shall call him, after the great black pitcher who reached the major leagues in middle age) distinguished me from his oppressors.

Satch had been appointed to the faculty of a Midwestern university after their new affirmative-action officer, who ironically was ousted long before my client, complained that the only blacks on the premises were tight ends and hurdlers on athletic scholarships. Satch was a rare find: a popular and fluent lecturer at a black college in Atlanta before he was located by a headhunter and tempted by the prestige of a white school with a national reputation. His sole flaw was that he'd never published even a recipe, and he made it quite clear to the reigning chairman of his new English department that he had no intention of doing so. There were enough yawns in print in his field already; besides, he confessed, he wasn't any good at cranking them out. I don't know why the chairman reassured him on this point— perhaps he was embarrassed by the government form he had to file listing the racial composition of his faculty, perhaps the affirmative-action man threatened a stink—but Satch was invited to join the Big Ten and quietly told not to worry, his teaching ability would be enough to ensure tenure.

Three years later a divided department voted against offering him a tenurial rank and failed to renew his contract. The vote was close, and Satch thought he could reverse it until he heard that the chairman had sealed his defeat by observing to his colleagues that tenure was unthinkable in their department without a record of steady appearance in learned journals. When accosted with his earlier representations, the chairman declined to remember and my enraged client slugged him. The punch was light, but the chairman hit a desk on his way to the floor. In the hubbub that followed, the chairman was hospitalized for a concussion and the student newspaper got wind of the assault. With the story out, charges were pressed; a local judge said Satch was a "role model" and sent him to jail for thirty days to mull over his behavior. By then, Satch desired only to get away from the university as quickly as possible; so he ordered me to let the appeal lapse. A few weeks later the novel about Africa arrived.

I've never heard from Satch since and don't know whether he returned to the black-college circuit, where he'd been reasonably happy before the talent scout scooped him up, or was ruined by the incident. I suspect the former. He was not a man given to pity, and there was a firmness about him that 1 could explain only by his Southern origins. He did not yet know where his place was, but he knew he had one somewhere, unlike so many Northern blacks who've made it. Indeed, Satch fumed not so much at his betrayal by the department chairman as at the absurdity of discharging an adroit classroom teacher (as everyone admitted he was) because he had nothing new to say in print about Milton. To add to the frustration, he thought tenure itself a feudal remnant—hut if whites could profit from it, he insisted, so should blacks.

I was pleased to get the book, though after a few chapters I was reading out of a sense of duty to a vanquished comrade. Then I came upon a particular scene, the symbolism of which was unshakable, even to its invading my life. It took place in a plane, the common literary encounter where a character, incident or even a line makes worthwhile three hundred pages of obedient slogging. Because of his rank as captain of industry, the businessman whose unraveling is the novel's thread must take long and tedious plane trips between Europe and Africa. On one of these journeys a young woman of a different class and hue enters the crowded plane with her mother and sister and takes the seat next to him. (The actual progression of the novel, and whether she was Indian or Portuguese, I don't remember, but my mind chiseled a cameo of the events that followed into a legend. I even dined out once or twice on the story.)

The young woman, hardly more than a girl, is not particularly pretty. After boarding the plane on its last European stop, she sits down with hardly a glance at the businessman. Then the stewardess passes out blankets to the dozing passengers, now settling down for the long night ahead, and soon the girl curls up in her seat. Their bodies touch, draw away and tentatively return. She places his hand on her thigh; he adjusts his blanket to confirm the message. Without speaking, they come closer, his fingers finding their way under her skirt, searching beneath a surprising array of undergarments until her dampness envelops him. Again and again he roams the depths between her legs, the plane trembling like an arrow in flight toward the heart of the continent. As the daylight glare fills the cabin, they disentangle below the mask of covers and prepare themselves for breakfast, only to come together again after the dishes have been removed. When the plane lands, they exchange a few meaningless sentences about her destination, their first words.

I read and reread the scene, at first because the mix of risk, transience and the unexpected seemed the very stuff of full-bodied eroticism. But soon I felt there was something about the setting in a complex machine moving above the earth at six hundred miles an hour that asked more of me than I could at that time know. I am a skittish flier, part of me often peering over the shoulder of the pilot, monitoring his dials, fussing with the radar, scanning the horizon. What seems like years aloft has taught me to observe the madman who keeps me aware of every sound and shake of the jet. I've come to recognize an absence of fear at takeoff or landing—the times when the aircraft is actually in greatest danger. It is in midflight, when vibrating hull and droning engines drug most passengers to sleep, that as a disbeliever in aerodynamic lift, distrustful of corporate responsibility, I must stay alert.

The scene in the novel seemed to me a wondrous invention, what fiction ought to be: totally plausible but beyond my imaginings, metaphor neither fully comprehensible nor easily forgettable. Still, I *did* forget it—made the scene mine and forgot—until several years later it happened to me. No, "happened to me" isn't quite right; I was not a passive participant. But the parallel to the book came to my mind immediately and drove me on to imitate art.

Late one afternoon Rudy and I were aimlessly talking shop when Bill Beveridge called and asked me to come to the coast to help head off the execution of Gary Gilmore. Though I've worked for enough killers to wonder at the depths of my perversity, I hadn't taken part in this case and knew only what was in the papers. Gilmore had wantonly murdered two unresisting men in robberies netting a few dollars and had left widows and children in his wake; he wanted to be shot; he had twice botched suicide attempts; he had dismissed his lawyers and managed to find counsel who agreed to serve his death wish, a fellow who was reported to own a share of the proceeds of publicizing what would inevitably be a Hollywood death. In turn, the lawyer was replaced by a literary agent.

Bill did not need help representing Gilmore's family or the apprehensive Death Row inmates in Utah who believed their lives would be placed in jeopardy by the execution, the first in many years. They had their own lawyers, after all. But in his role as the Good Works man in California, Bill needed someone to go to Salt Lake City and persuade the newly elected governor that Gilmore's death would be a circus. It was his notion that the governor could be made to see that killing Gilmore on national television, with hundreds of reporters from Reuters, Tass and the domestic wire services observing, would be bad for his administration, for Mormons and for Utah. Surely such a cockeyed idea—though elsewhere it had worked—had been tried here and failed? Nevertheless, Bill was optimistic. On the phone he always talks quickly, urgently, as if he must get out of a burning building as soon as he hangs up; I couldn't say no to him. Rudy and I dashed to the car he keeps in an underground garage for a monthly fee that would support an entire Peruvian village, and roared out like the Green Hornet. He waited while I packed, then deposited me at Kennedy in time for a late flight to San Francisco just as they were turning off the metal detectors for the night.

Errands like this were hardly unusual; sending lawyers around the country armed with intricate constitutional submissions was the way Good Works had kept executioners out of work for a decade. But as I caught my breath, stowing a briefcase in the compartment above an aisle seat, I hadn't the foggiest notion of what I would say to the governor, much less to the staff I would have to hurdle in order to get to him. Not having a client, I thought as the plane lumbered from the gate, I would have to devise a way of presenting the Good Works position as the public interest. Of my own interest I wasn't sure. If Gilmore wanted to die, why not let him? A gory televised death might be just what was needed to cool off the pols who— though most of them knew better—blathered a couple of paragraphs about how a few executions would reduce violence whenever constituents complained of crime in the streets. This was deceitful; they knew it and I knew it, and while tolerating my own tricks—always to such noble ends—I could not abide falsehood in the leadership.

At any rate, if someone had to go, Gilmore seemed highly qualified for the post. He wanted to die, and who was to say he didn't have good reasons? His life had been a wasteland of cruelty, both taken and given. He'd spent eighteen of the last twenty-one years in prison. Letters to his girlfriend suggested that when rage overtook him, he would kill again if given the opportunity. He wasn't insane—at least the *Times* didn't think so, and for all their faults the editors of that esteemed journal have their fingers clenched on the pulse of normality. But my own doubts would have to be put aside. My loyalty was to abolition—or at least to that part of my professional self that had labored long in its behalf. If Bill thought this killing might spur another governor to gain a few points in the Harris poll by cleaning out his Death Row, then I would have to perform.

These thoughts were leading me to *the* lawyer's question—after the talk, after feelings have been ventilated and reservations put aside, ideas rated, strategies examined, interest groups placated; after the rituals, consultations and coffee breaks, what do we do?—when I noticed the woman behind the book. Dressed in a wheat-colored, loose-fitting blouse and a wide print skirt, she literally flowed toward the empty seat between us. Framing an open face, high cheeks, a spectacularly flat, almost Indian nose fell ringlets of curly hair that tripped over her ears and brow and down the side of her neck. I was overcome. Such is the wonder of the human brain and the folly of our dim apprehension of its workings that immediately I yearned for a hijacker to order the jet to Guatemala, where she and I could live among the pineapples, never to return to this life.

She looked up and took me in for a moment, only to hand me the ticket that had slipped from a jacket pocket as I hurriedly pulled off my coat. Back she went to a book of stories by Flannery O'Connor, a choice revealing at once that I had lodged my fantasy at a four-peaker with a red rocking chair and a view—in the language the Michelin people use to describe the cream of cozy, out-of-the-way European hostelries. I grabbed a reprint and pretended to read, but it was all prop; the print swam. We did not talk until the pilot reported the ecstasy that United felt at having us aboard. As we reached an invisible Lake Erie off the right wing, her book slapped shut and the article fell to my lap; we brushed away the seat belts, turned toward each other, and it all tumbled out.

The South African businessman's transit had been wordless, but ours bubbled with chatter. His liaison crossed ethnic, class and cultural lines, whereas we were twins separated before memory, rediscovering a common past. Where he had to weigh risk—the girl might expose him with a scream—against pleasure, we were already lovers, preoccupied with each other, fearless. Near Chicago we moved closer, the only benign association I have for that bitter, ungiving place where once my lungs gagged with gas. Thighs pressing, heads bent in and slightly forward, we giggled and whispered, laughed and shrugged. By Omaha, afraid of missing even a syllable of this language of love, we found it impossible to look away. Mates and work, children and childhood raced out. We hung on each pause, sigh and smile, on the twitches of recollection accompanying a lover taken or lost, a dying parent, a bout with therapy, the story of a project accepted by a for-once-rewarding world only after it bad ceased to hold our attention.

When we had stripped and laid bare all that could be told, we lapsed into silence. 1 caressed her body beneath the tangled blankets. She pressed, pinched, fondled and explored me with every gentle variation known to my sense of touch. When the pilot announced that the darkness below was California, agitation seized us. Breathing as hard as privacy would allow, we set to it, bringing each other off with a frankness that could not have been greater were we safe in a king-size bed in a cavernous hotel, out of season on a storm-isolated island in the North Sea. We had to have this to take away at the end of the journey.

As the plane bounced over the Sierras and slid down toward San Francisco Bay, under the blankets, clothes askew, limbs entangled, we lay there spent. At the landing we exchanged wistful glances and reluctantly pulled apart, an act I remember as comparable to separating two pieces of adhesive tape. When we left the plane, the stewardess babbled the obligatory goodbye: "I hope you enjoyed your United flight," Yes, I thought. Yes.

To be with her until the last, I told the driver to drop her off at her destination on Lombard Street before taking me to the Cliff House. It was one of those mint-condition San Francisco Victorians, placed where this most precipitous of all streets seems to topple into the Bay. She stepped from the cab, and a man appeared and took her bag, a man I now knew, though we had never met. They smiled at each other but did not kiss. As the driver pulled from the curb, she leaned toward the half-open window and waved: "Good luck with your case." I whimpered all the way to the hotel.

Early the next morning I awoke with an enormous appetite for motion that sent me tearing through the hills and valleys of downtown San Francisco like Bill Rodgers. Obviously experienced distance men emerged from their nonchalant stride long enough to throw a quick you'll-be-sorry look in my direction as I took Nob Hill at a gallop; hoping that the woman on the 747 would jog out from Grant Avenue as I passed, fall into step and race beside me to the top of the hill, I never felt the pain.

By the time I saw Bill Beveridge, his tactics had shifted. He'd concluded that there was no hope of a statehouse postponement. His only chance now to thwart the execution was a lawyer he dispatched to Salt Lake City who thought a federal judge could be persuaded to reinstate the lapsed appeal. He dragged me to a room in the Fairmont where he'd agreed to meet the press, the only source of influence left to him. By capturing a few seconds on the tube for a condemnation of sensational media coverage of Gilmore's impending date with the firing squad, he might deter a general bloodletting in Texas or Florida. He is not one to chew over irony.

Bill read his statement, then reread it for the cameras. Reporters flipped through the text of a news release, asked him whether homicide rates were climbing, how many seconds after impact it would take Gilmore to die and what he thought of an eye for an eye. While he fielded their solemn questions, I sat blankly staring at the folding chairs filled with journalists, imagining she would walk into the room and lead me out of the hotel to the sports car Dustin Hoffman drove in *The Graduate*. We'd head for the Mendocino coast and a ride that would never end.

When Bill called on me to answer a query about deterrence, it took several moments of throat-clearing to snap out of the daydream. "The irony," I opined, hiding my distraction behind professorial disdain, "resides in the fact that capital punishment makes it harder to convict the guilty of violent crimes. Whenever the death penalty is a potential sanction, the accused will go to trial and thereby dilute the state's already thin prosecutorial muscle."

"But, Professor," a man asked, pronouncing the word as if it were a synonym for shmuck, "what are we going to do with these animals? Keep them locked up at taxpayer expense? Please comment on the warden's estimate that it would cost sixty-five thousand a year to maintain Gilmore in a cell."

I sat down before he finished. In the awkward silence that followed, another reporter mercifully interjected a question about the ethics of Gilmore's last lawyer. Bill resumed control of the meeting while I returned to woolgathering. I'd been to the jagged coast before, but never to the Oregon border; what would happen when we reached it?

I knew something had to be done to break the grip of fantasy and self-absorption, fast hardening into sentimentality. I could see it in Bill's confusion as we left the room. He'd turned the key in the ignition, only to have the motor crash from its props to the ground. Having known me exclusively as a worker, he couldn't square this zombie with the person he thought he knew. Coming out of it, I calmed my bewildered friend: "Trouble at home."

This reassured him, as it would anyone; it is sufficient explanation for any behavioral oddity. He relaxed and resumed his madcap schedule of rounds to save the life of a man who wanted to die and whom he disliked intensely.

Then I did something for which I was totally unprepared—did it immediately because there never would be time enough for preparing. I called Connie and described everything that happened. I told her I was prompted not by guilt or pride, but simply by the need to be to her what I was to myself. Stretched out on the broad hotel double bed, phone cradled against my shoulder, I rubbed my eyes in disbelief. She had caught my tone perfectly; she was saying to herself, but also to me, "It was worth waiting for."

Once I thought I saw the woman on the 747 standing on Forty-fifth Street near Shubert Alley during the intermission of a Broadway musical, but as I approached, a strange face turned in my direction. A few months ago my secretary took a mysterious phone message from a woman who said she would call again and never did. I wondered if she had tracked me down. Not that it matters. I am always curious about the present of my past, but the longing failed to survive my confession. The desire fled before the reality I imposed, but the metaphor of the woman remained. My mind has drilled the experience to order and marched it around to the point where now I feel our encounter was no accidental brush of bodies. Whatever condition of existence challenged the novelist's imagination also provoked me. The woman and I had not imitated art; we had responded to a circumstance that when exposed to a writer led to a scene, and when exposed to others led to life.

Hurtling through space that offers no resistance is the source of my flier's anxiety. To avoid the nothingness of flight, I desperately urge the irrepressible force of the giant jet, wide-bodied like the woman, toward a collision with an immovable object. Despite my preference for death to dissolution, the aircraft refuses to comply. At midflight cruising speed I perceive the plane as without inhibition. My malaise, my happy lack of adjustment to the facts, is that I expect and wish entropy. Flying is an infinite regression, numbers counted backwards endlessly, that I must impede. Otherwise, I am faced with a loss of self.

The love-testing, soul-searching crisis peaks at such moments—when we believe, in iron-clad deception, that there is nothing to stop us. Freud's patients were cured by letting go, but their children must hold on, resist and desist. In the cylinder of the 747 I felt defenseless and watched boundaries crumble. To counteract the tendency toward dissolution, the flying apart, I sought the resistance that a strange other, even a compliant one, always presents. That's the trick: to find the difficulty that matters and embrace it. In a room full of danger, take a chair next to the person who threatens you most.

Resistance, then, is not be denied or plowed through or analyzed away; it should be welcomed aboard and given its place. Perhaps my takes are short because an inner governor looks after me, switches me on and off, blocks the way, then opens a door, pushes me out and pulls me back, perceiving through its mysterious circuitry that longer takes will leave me flaccid. The works in this black box are invisible, but I know they are there the way a physicist knows of quarks: by the results. Without resistance I would take the easy way, the way of generality, laziness and habit, unaccountable and uncounting—the moral landscape as free of friction as the thin air and empty space passed through by the monster jet. I must have opposition to keep from loving the reflection of my special case, from becoming a covert worshiper of my own quirky, omnivorous nature.

Of the Gilmore execution, I am not a reliable witness. Anyone concerned about precision must check the accuracy of my version against the press reports, of which there are many. Preoccupied by changing before my own eyes, distracted by the unfamiliar, monolithic desert space, there to gape rather than work, I am afraid I saw the movie of Gilmore's killing even before they cast the lead. I do remember—how could I forget?—that afterwards I was ready to be judged and thereby to judge. Not until two years later, after Slade's phone call, did it sink in, but I had seen the worst that our need for order could do and I still wanted to be part of it. At last I was ready to abide by the rules without giving an easy inch to their built-in inequities and cunning iniquities.

Only fragments remain. Twenty of us were bused to a bunker and handed cotton for our ears. We stood in a cinderblock shed, in a ragged line behind a slanting wooden barricade. Down the road the state police herded pickets, priests, tourists and reporters found unworthy by the press officer of the Bureau of Prisons. Gilmore wore white pants and sneakers, white paper heart pinned to his black T-shirt; the blood fled from one heart to the other. Was there dignity in this monster's last command, or does our romance-corrupted view of the world make it impossible to know? They say he said "Let's do it" before the warden's nod sent a volley of shots thunderclapping against the walls of the shed. But we, the official observers, aren't really sure; with cotton in our ears, we don't even know the facts.

During these last months there have been many false starts, many hesitations while I've felt for pressure points, the right counterweight to my own will against which to drop my shoulder and push hard without crashing through to nothingness. Now I act closer to the history of my feelings. With proper regrets, my ambitious former student has heard that I'm too scattered for academic budgetry. Fritz accepts that there is too much tightness for fiction. Sam will have to stick it out alone. Clare has gracefully bowed to some lawyerly line drawing: half my time goes to her system, half to my own frolics and diversions.

As for the judgeship, I drew up a long list of sensible and imaginative stratagems to get it, and spent several weeks playing them out. I revised my resume, let the good senator who was responsible for the choice know there were those who firmly believed I would not subvert the republic, and ran an adroit, cautious but thoroughly vigorous campaign—even to deploying the Soft Killer to bend an ear or two. But now the staggered flash, the cutting in and out, of these reconstructions has given me what I want. Not the gavel of the mighty—that's up to the fates—but the certainty of my own pace: still hurtling through this abrupt, deflecting city, brushing friends as I go, but now feeling for the thread that binds and connects my blip, blip, blip, my uptown, downtown, East Side, West Side, all around the town, my no-longer ego but very much my own blip, blip, blip.

About the Author

Michael Meltsner began his career as counsel to the NAACP Legal Defense Fund in the 1960s and then taught at the Columbia Law School. In the 1980s he served as dean of the Northeastern Law School in Boston where he is currently the Matthews Distinguished University Professor of Law. His memoir, *The Making of a Civil Rights Lawyer*, was published in 2006 (University of Virginia Press). Among his other writings are *Cruel and Unusual: The Supreme Court and Capital Punishment* (2nd edition 2011, Quid Pro Books) and *In Our Name: A Play of the Torture Years* (2011). He lives in Cambridge, Massachusetts.

Visit us at *www.quidprobooks.com*.